Canada
Province Studies

Written By
RANDY L. WOMACK, M.Ed.
Learning Disabilities & Behavior Disorders
Illustrated By
CHRISTINA "Chris" LEW

Cover Design: **WOMACK & LEW**

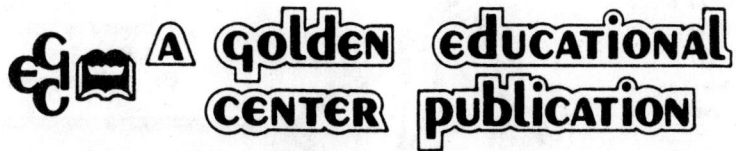

857 Lake Blvd.
Redding, California 96003

To Teachers and Parents

This book, *Canada Province Studies*, was written as a simplified, yet complete, resource book for you to use. The activities can be used as a supplemental resource for your regular history, social studies and/or geography curriculum. It is also a great overview to use when teaching foreign languages.

There are fifteen separate sections in this book. The first section is a group of supplemental maps to be used throughout the book. The second section is an overview of Canada. The next twelve sections are about the provinces and territories in Canada. Each of the provinces/territories and Canada sections has a large 8 1/2 x 11" map, a one page current fact/information sheet (1991 Almanac), a short one or two page history through independence and one page of review questions. There are also bonus activities/questions that some of your students can do with another resource book. The fifteenth section is an answer key for the review questions.

New vocabulary words are introduced at the beginning of each section. If your students are capable of looking up the words in a dictionary, please have them do so. You might even have them use the words in their own sentences. It is suggested that you, as the teacher, go over the words with your students <u>before</u> the lessons are actually begun, making sure that the meanings are understood by the children. This will help your students grasp the concepts being taught.

We hope you can elaborate on our brief historical discussions. Finding current information about the various provinces of Canada can help make the historical events your students read about more meaningful. Canada is a very important country in North America; and our historical sections should act as catalysts to study present-day events and attitudes in Canada.

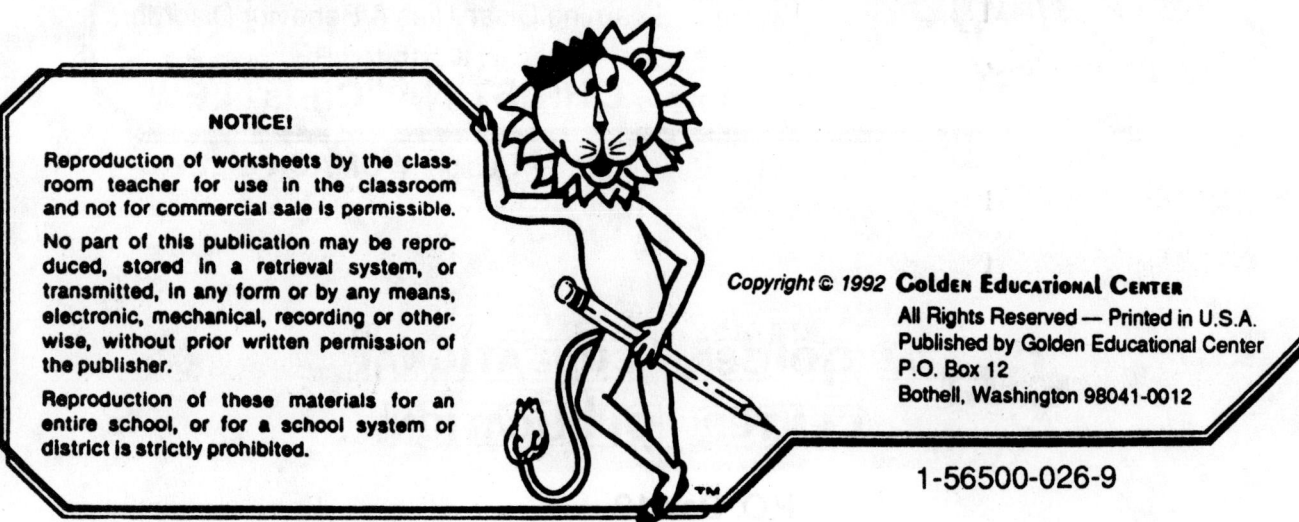

NOTICE!

Reproduction of worksheets by the classroom teacher for use in the classroom and not for commercial sale is permissible.

No part of this publication may be reproduced, stored in a retrieval system, or transmitted, in any form or by any means, electronic, mechanical, recording or otherwise, without prior written permission of the publisher.

Reproduction of these materials for an entire school, or for a school system or district is strictly prohibited.

Copyright © 1992 **Golden Educational Center**
All Rights Reserved — Printed in U.S.A.
Published by Golden Educational Center
P.O. Box 12
Bothell, Washington 98041-0012

1-56500-026-9

CANADA
Section Contents

Section One . . . . **EXTRA MAPS**
Section Two . . . . **CANADA**

PROVINCES

Section Three . . . . **ALBERTA**
Section Four . . . . **BRITISH COLUMBIA**
Section Five . . . . **MANITOBA**
Section Six . . . . **NEW BRUNSWICK**
Section Seven . . . . **NEWFOUNDLAND**
Section Eight . . . . **NOVA SCOTIA**
Section Nine . . . . **ONTARIO**
Section Ten . . . . **PRINCE EDWARD ISLAND**
Section Eleven . . . . **QUEBEC**
Section Twelve . . . . **SASKATCHEWAN**

TERRITORIES

Section Thirteen . . . . **NORTHWEST TERRITORIES**
Section Fourteen . . . . **YUKON TERRITORY**

ANSWER KEYS

Section Fifteen . . . . **ANSWER KEYS**

EXTRA MAPS

Historical • Geographical & Political Maps

Order of Maps in This Section.

1. Rupert's Land
2. Hudson's Bay Territory
3. Early French Settlements
4. Upper & Lower Canada
5. Growth of Canada
6. Political Boundaries
7. Major Waterways

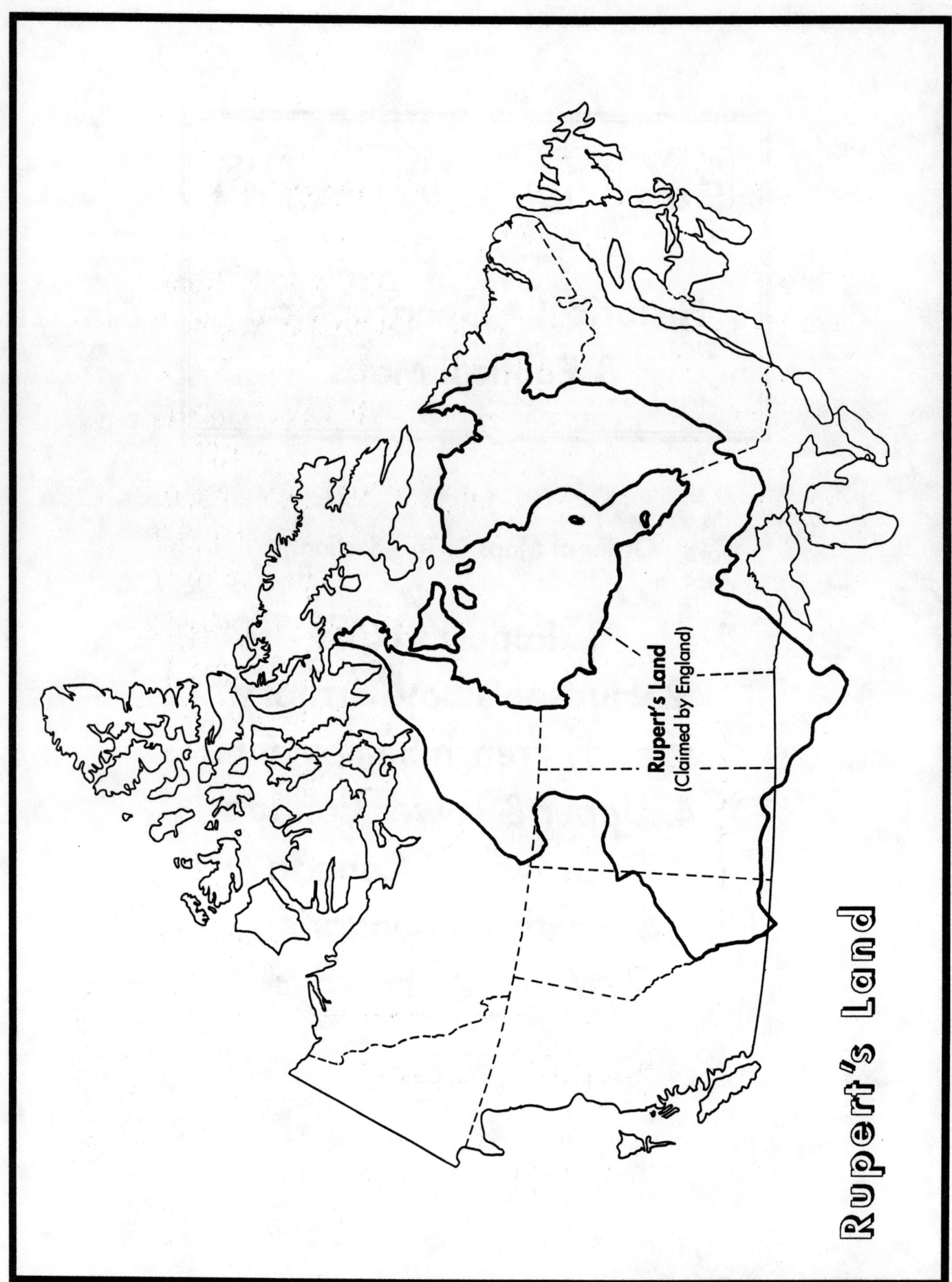

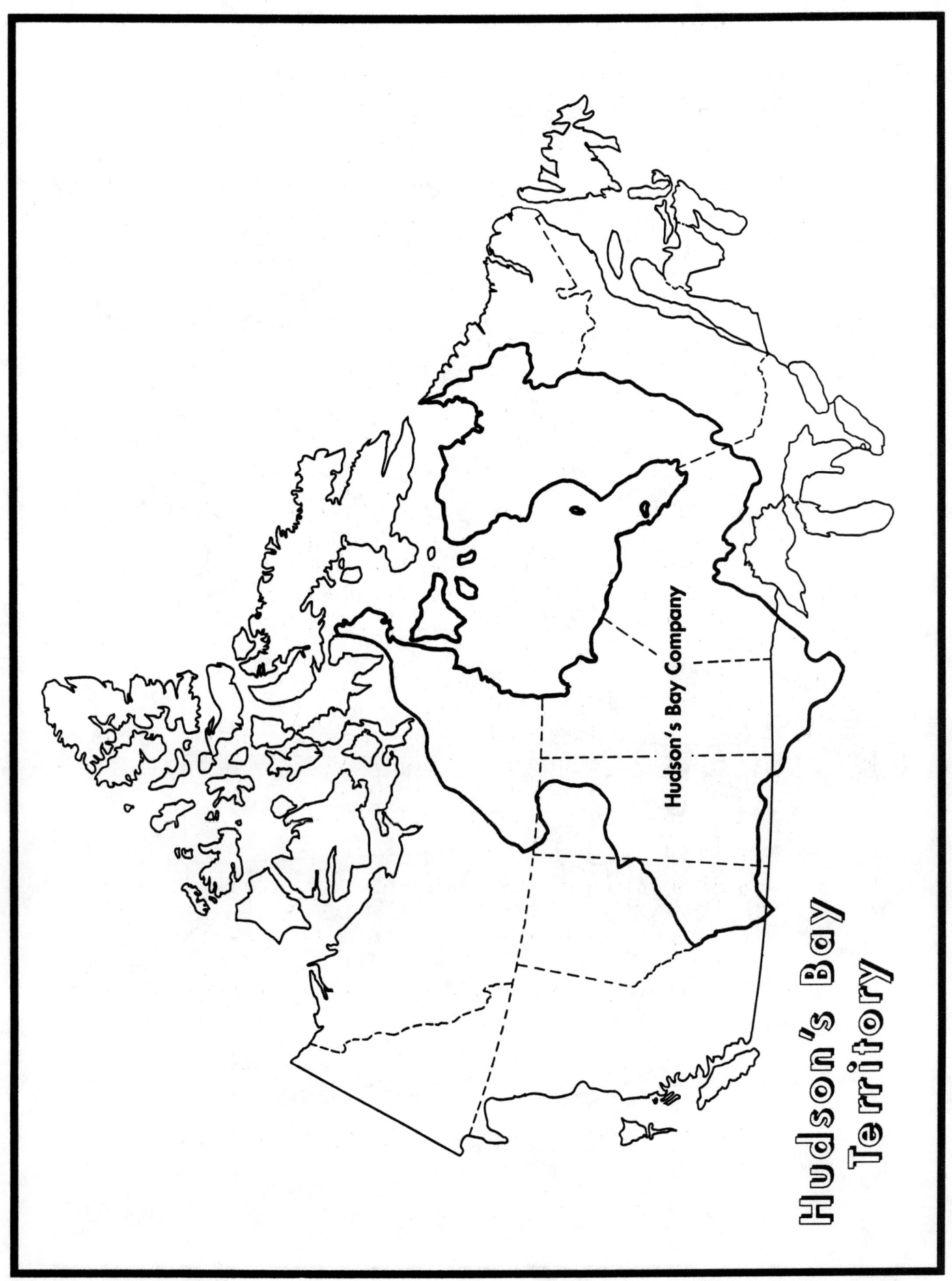

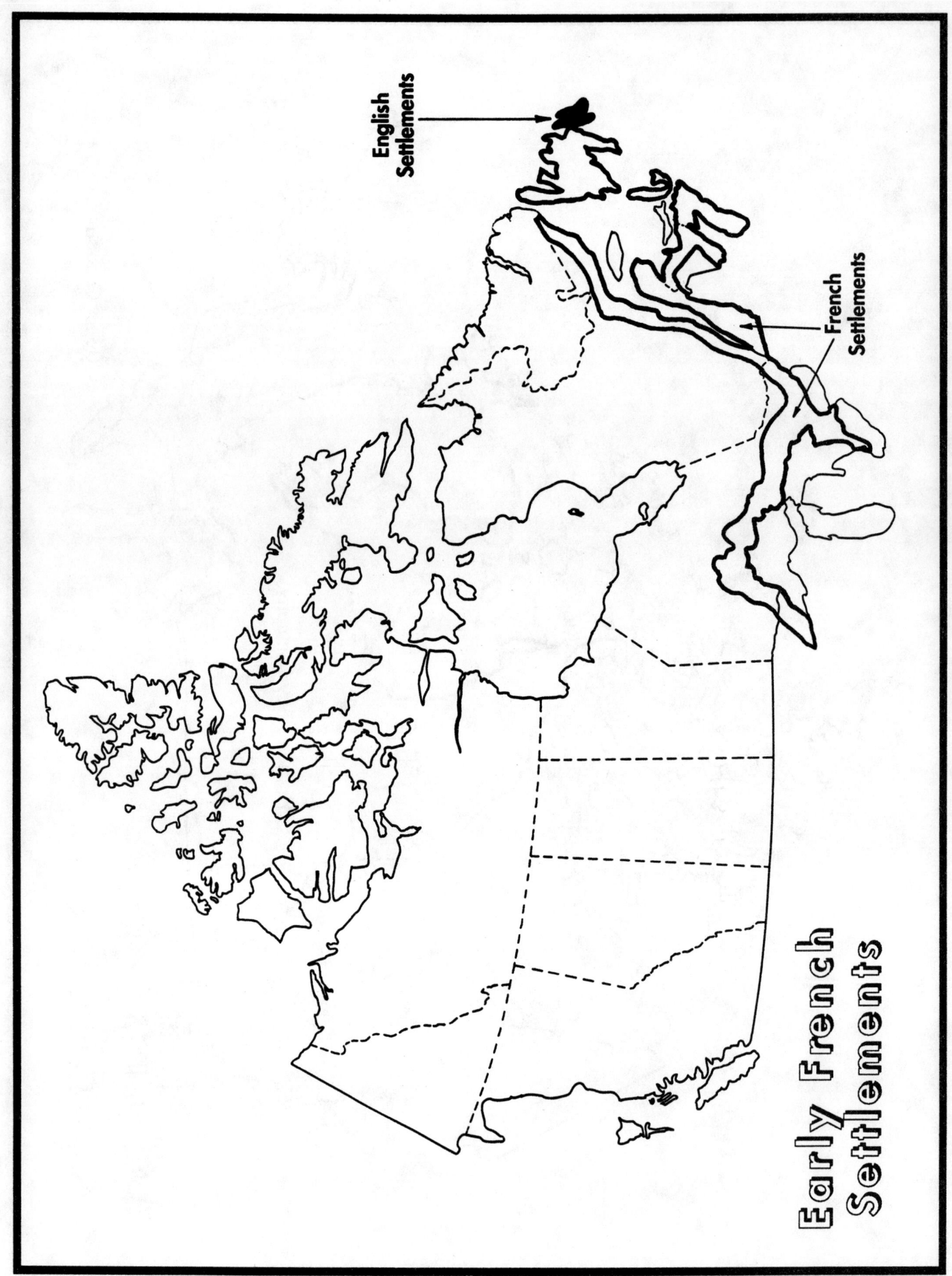

CANADA: Section 1 – 4

© Golden Educational Center

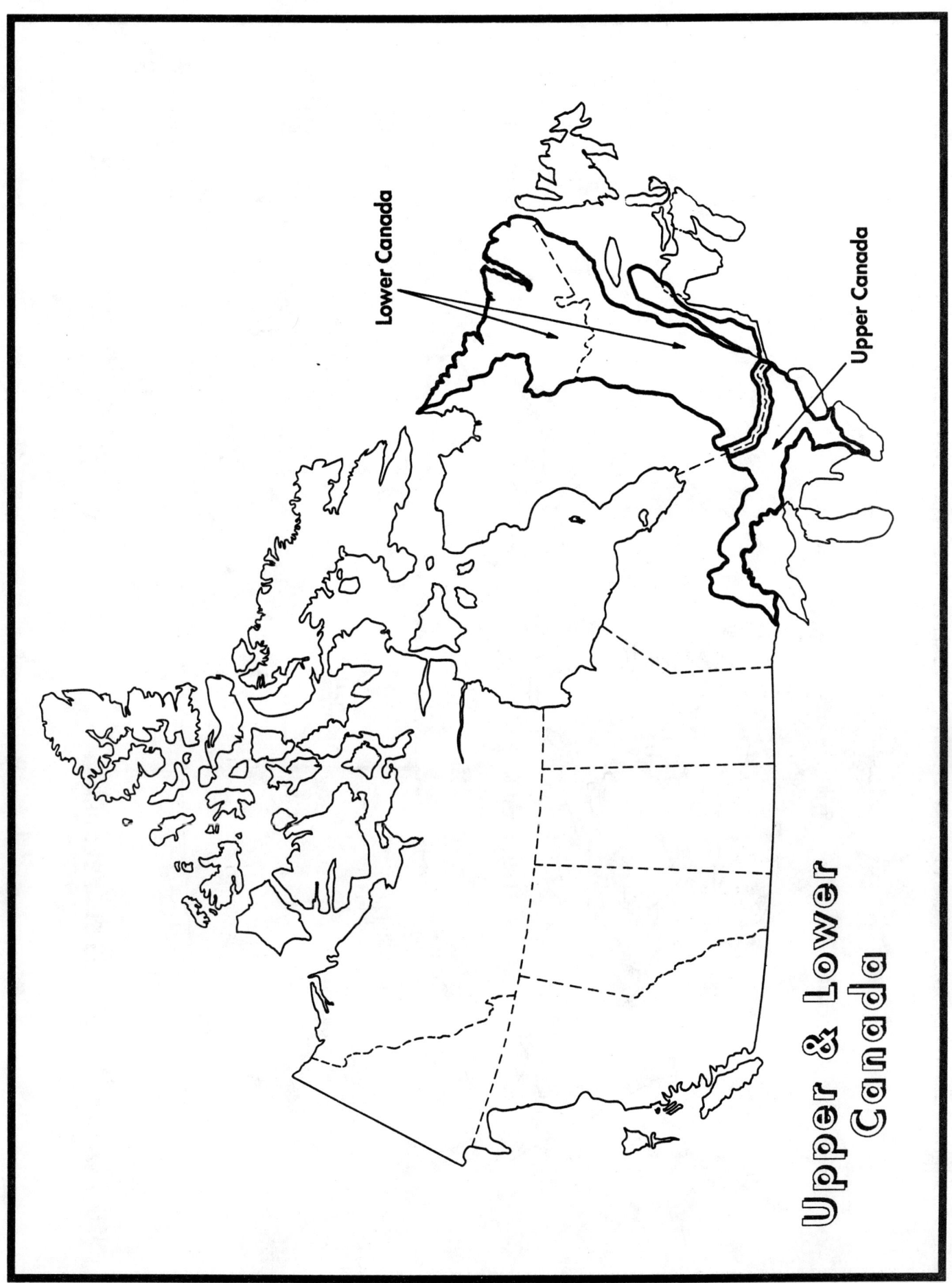

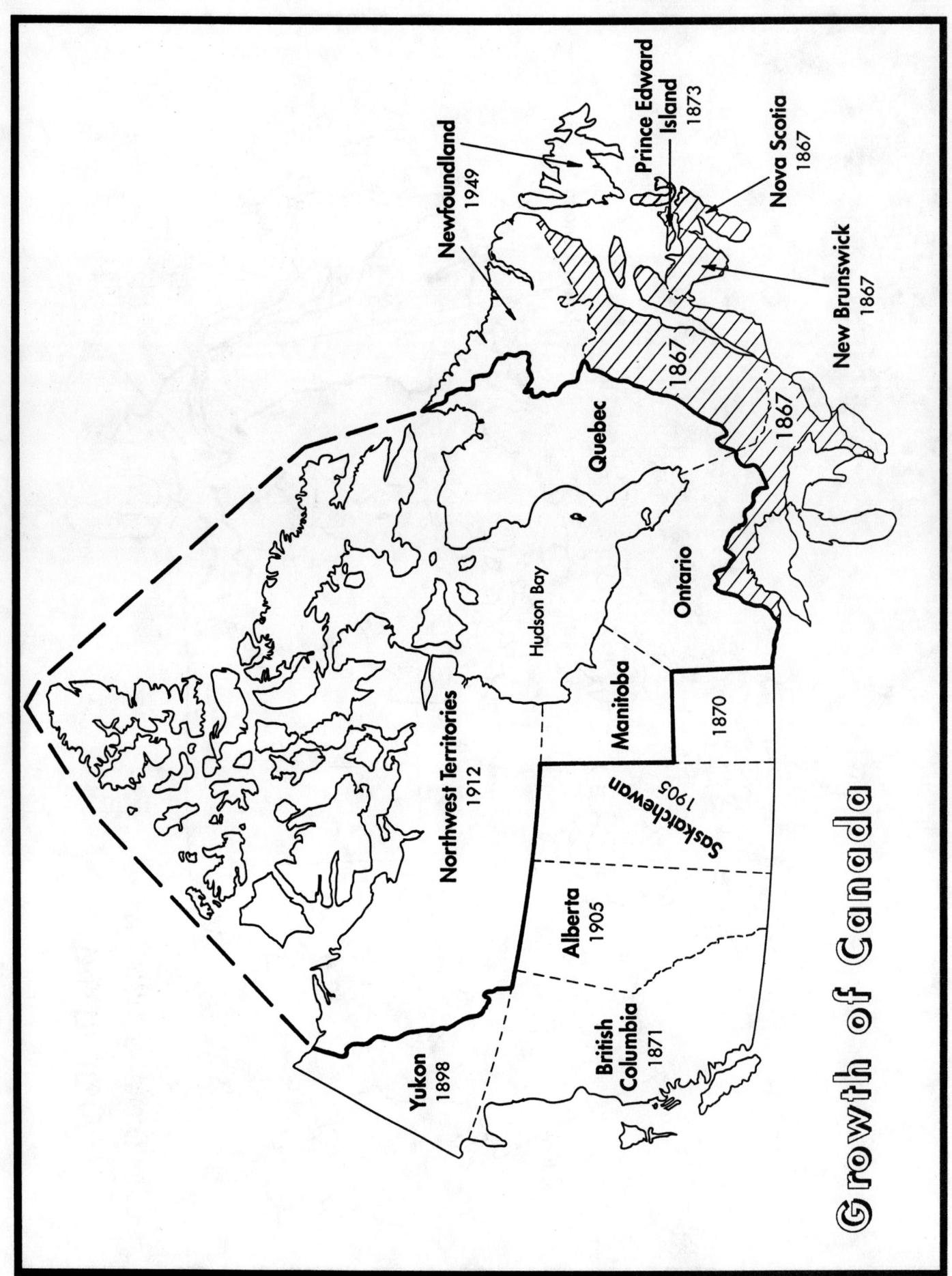

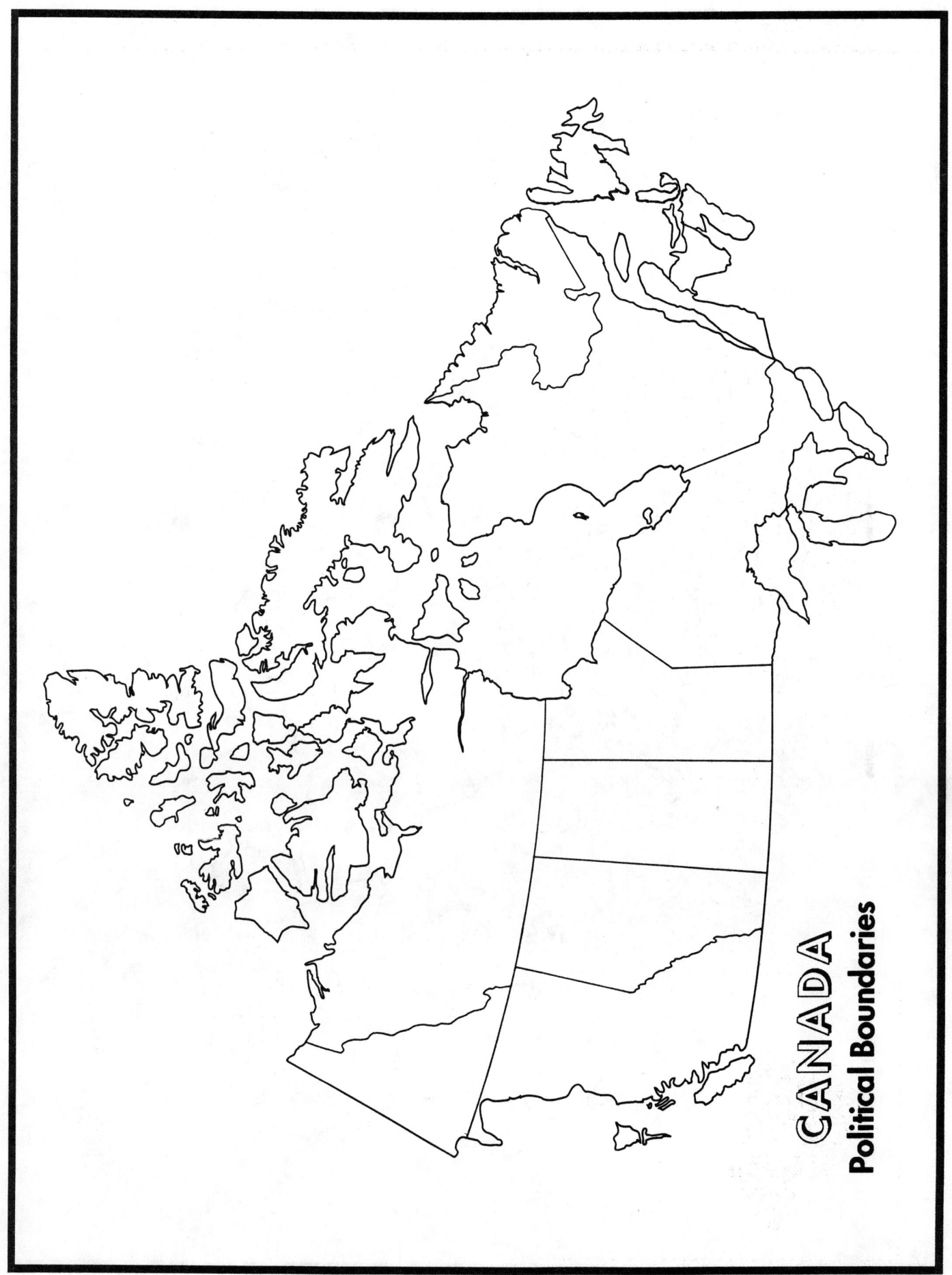

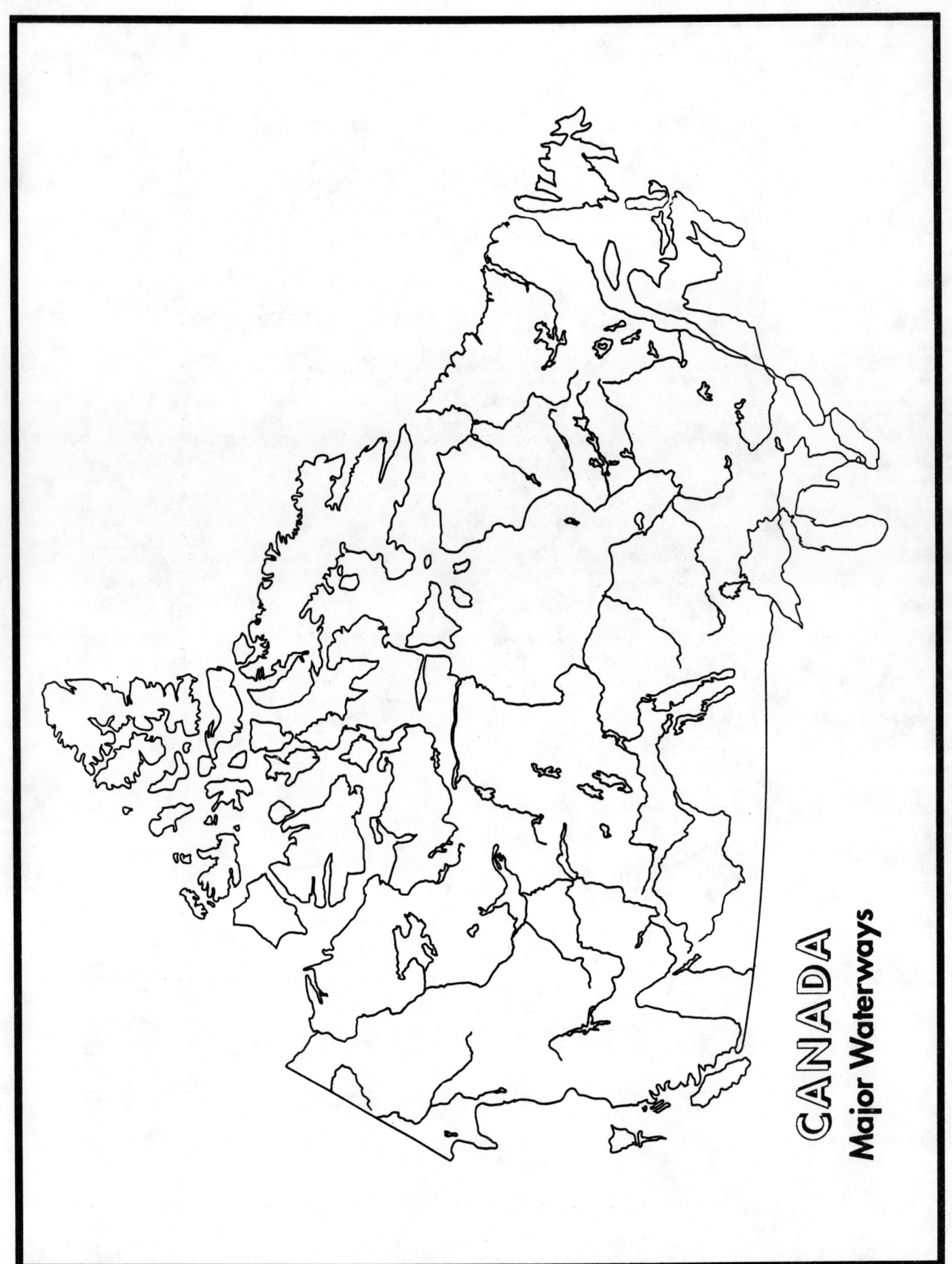

CANADA

Map • Facts • History & Review Questions

New Words to Learn:
Find the words in a dictionary and write the meanings on the lines.

1. **ancestor** - _____
2. **conference** - _____
3. **constitution** - _____
4. **convention** - _____
5. **democracy** - _____
6. **Dominion** - _____
7. **escalate** - _____
8. **foothold** - _____
9. **interior** - _____
10. **province** - _____
11. **royal** - _____
12. **tribe** - _____

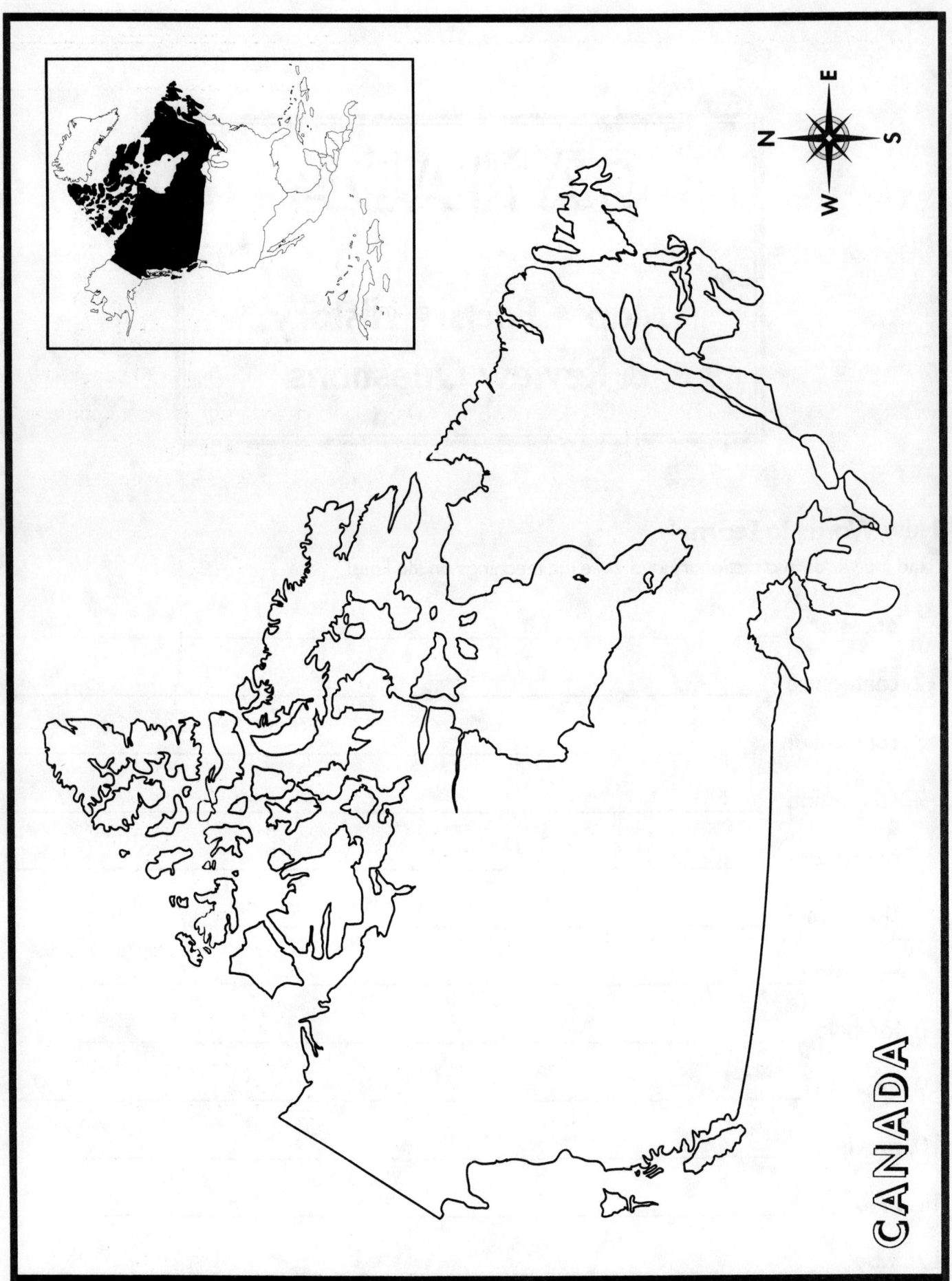

CANADA: Section 2 - 10

CANADA
(KAN-uh-duh)

Name ――――――――――

Date ――――――――――

DATE of INDEPENDENCE: July 1, 1931.

NATION'S CAPITAL CITY: Ottawa.

OFFICIAL LANGUAGES: English and French.

FORM of GOVERNMENT: Confederation with Parliamentary **Democracy**.

AREA: 9,215,426 square kilometers   (3,558,096 square miles).

POPULATION (est.1991): 26,527,000 people.   <u>Density</u>: 3 people per square kilometer.
7 people per square mile.
76% urban (city) living and 24% rural (country) living.

LARGEST CITY: Toronto - 3,427,000 people.

ELEVATION: <u>Highest</u>: Mount Logan - 5,950 meters (19,520 feet).
<u>Lowest</u>: Sea level.

ADDITIONAL INFORMATION: The country of Canada stretches South from the North Pole to the U.S. border. Because of Canada's cold northern climate, 85% of the population lives in the southernmost regions— within 200 miles of the U.S. and Canadian border. • Canada is the second largest country in the world. Only the U.S.S.R has more area. • Canada's wealth of natural resources is considered its greatest possession.

Canada's Flag

Flag Description

1. The two end sections are red and the middle section is white.

2. The eleven pointed maple leaf in the middle is red. It is one of Canada's national symbols.

3. Color the flag the correct colors.

© Golden Educational Center

CANADA: **Section 2 - 11**

CANADA

Name _____

Date _____

EARLY HISTORY in BRIEF

Indian **tribes** lived throughout Canada long before any white people arrived. Most of the tribes hunted and fished in areas that later became large Canadian cities. They called a portion of the Saint Lawrence River valley *Canada*, from an Indian word that meant a *'group of huts.'*

Vikings from Iceland were the first known white men to visit the eastern shores of Canada in the A.D. 1000's. There is evidence that they established a settlement in northern Newfoundland at L'Anse aux Meadows. The English explorer, John Cabot, sailed from England in 1497. Historians believe he landed on Newfoundland or Cape Breton Island.

In 1524, an Italian, Giovanni da Verrazano, explored the Canadian coast for France. Ten years later the French explorer, Jacques Cartier became the first European to reach the Gulf of Saint Lawrence. He claimed the surrounding area for France. A year later he sailed up the Saint Lawrence River as far inland as where Montreal is today. France paid little attention to Canada during the rest of the 1500's.

The French explorer, Samuel de Champlain, is often called the *Father of New France*. (The French called their North American colonies *New France*.) In 1608, he founded Quebec, establishing the first permanent settlement in Canada. He explored the **interior** as far as the Georgian Bay on Lake Huron. Montreal was first named Ville Marie and was founded as a missionary center in 1642.

King Louis XIV made Canada a **province** of France in 1663. Within one hundred years there were about 60,000 French settlers in Canada. They became the **ancestors** of today's French Canadians.

As a **royal** colony under French rule, the settlers had many hardships. They had to defend themselves against the Dutch, English and Iroquois Indians. Compte de Frontenac was appointed governor of the colony by the King of France. He became a leader in the fight against the Indians until the early 1700's.

From the first years of settlement, the colonists from France and New England began fighting over the rich fur trade in the Canadian territory. However, the fighting **escalated** in 1689. The Hudson's Bay Company gained a **foothold** for England on Hudson Bay in 1670. The French colony of Louisiana was established in 1699. The French then built a chain of forts to link Louisiana to New France. Great Britain gained control of Nova Scotia, Newfoundland and the Hudson Bay region as part of the *Treaty of Utrecht* in 1713. For the next 30 years there was peace in New France. This was the longest period of peace in the history of New France.

CANADA

Name _____

Date _____

The final struggle between France and Great Britain began in 1758. The United States refers to this struggle as the *French and Indian War*. Europeans refer to this as the *Seven Years' War*. The French were winning until 1758, when the British soldiers gained control of key French positions in the interior and also captured Louisbourg. In 1759, British forces defeated the French at the Battle of Quebec. A year later, the French surrendered the colony of Montreal. Great Britain gained control of Canada in the *Treaty of Paris* in 1763. France received control of Saint Pierre and the Miquelon Islands.

The British made very few changes in the life and government of the colony. However, Canada was renamed the *Province of Quebec*. The Revolutionary War in the 13 American colonies left the British leaders fearful they would lose their colonies in Canada unless they ruled firmly. In the War of 1812, the Canadians defeated the invasions of the United States. After the war, the Canadian colonists sought self-government.

The British government sent Lord Durham to Canada to study the troubles and unrest in Canada. From Lord Durham's suggestion, in 1848, the British granted Canada limited self-government.

The *Quebec **Conference** of 1864* turned out to be a **constitutional convention**. The representatives who attended were called the "Fathers of Confederation." Some of the representatives wanted to call the new government the *Kingdom of Canada*. However, the name **Dominion** of *Canada* was finally chosen. *The British North America Act* was passed by the British Parliament in 1867, joining the provinces of Canada, including New Brunswick, and Nova Scotia; and forming Ontario and Quebec. It was not until July 1, 1931, that Canada became a totally independent country. ❑

The Canadian Coat of Arms

The Canadian Coat of Arms has red maple leaves below the royal arms of England, Scotland, Ireland and France.

© GOLDEN EDUCATIONAL CENTER

CANADA: **Section 2** - 13

CANADA

Name _____

REVIEW QUESTIONS   Date _____

Fill in the blanks with the correct answer.

1. Canada's largest city according to population is _____ .

2. In 1867, the British North America Act joined _____, _____, and _____ and formed _____ and Quebec.

3. _____ and _____ are the official languages of Canada.

4. Vikings from _____ were the _____ known white men to visit the eastern shores of Canada (North America) around the year _____ .

5. What was the year Canada become an independent country? _____

6. Explain how Canada got its name and what it means.
   _____
   _____
   _____

7. Why were the British leaders so insistent on ruling Canada firmly?
   _____
   _____
   _____

8. Explain the struggle (and outcome) over Canada between France and England.
   _____
   _____
   _____

9. List the names of Canada from the time the French first explored the territory.
   _____
   _____

Bonus ☆ ☆ ☆

Use another resource book and write a report on the Vikings, Lord Durham, the Seven Year's War, the War of 1812, the Revolutionary War or the British North America Act. Include pictures and maps in your report if they are applicable.

CANADA: Section 2 - 14   © Golden Educational Center

ALBERTA

Map • Facts • History & Review Questions

New Words to Learn:
Find the words in a dictionary and write the meanings on the lines.

1. **ally** - _____
2. **compete** - _____
3. **descent** - _____
4. **geographer** - _____
5. **merge** - _____
6. **missionary** - _____
7. **plain** - _____
8. **prairie** - _____
9. **premier** - _____
10. **promote** - _____
11. **survey** - _____

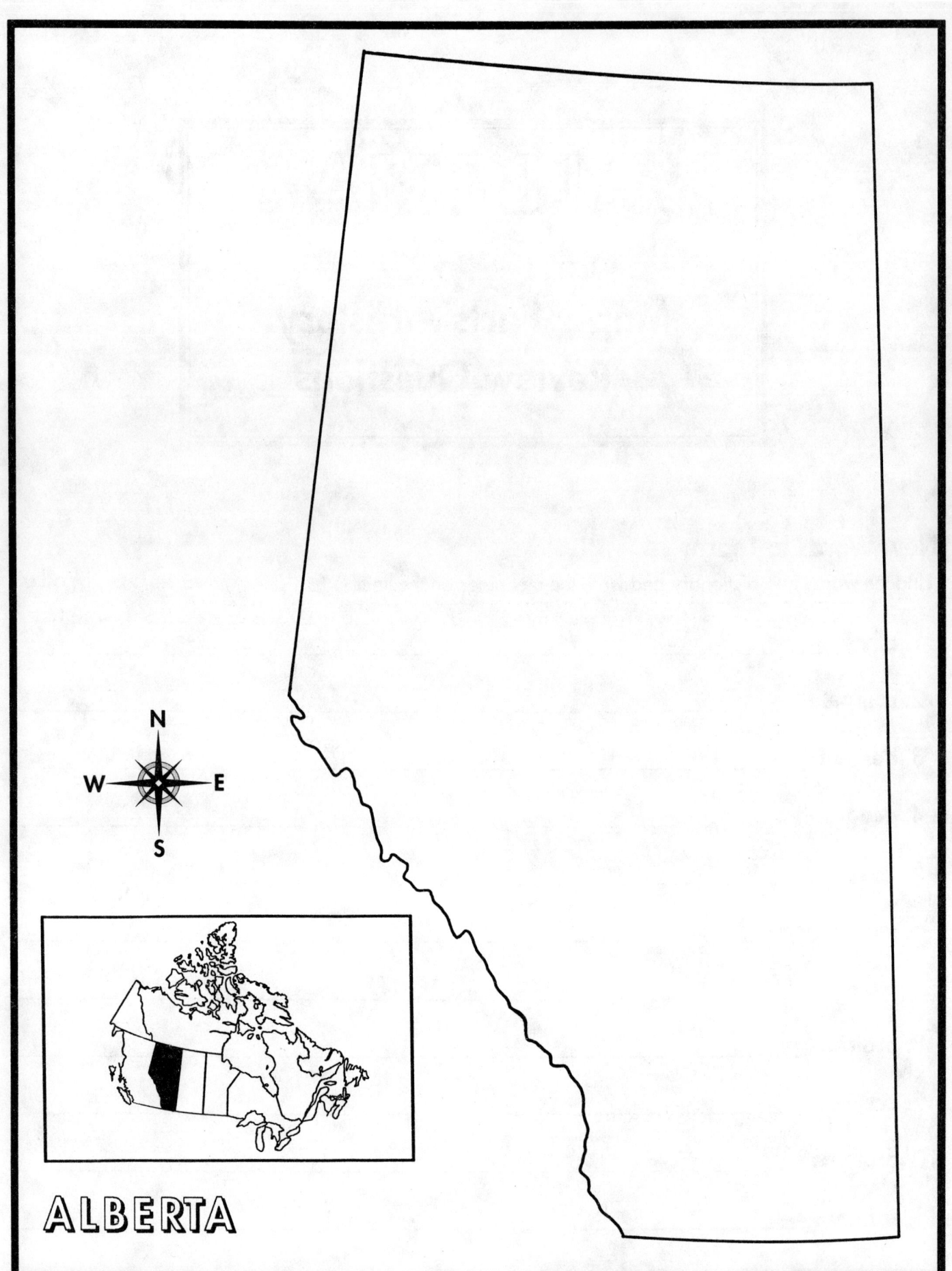

ALBERTA
(AL–bur–tuh)

Name _____

Date _____

BECAME A PROVINCE: September 1, 1905 — the 8th province.

CAPITAL CITY: Edmonton.

AREA: 644,389 square kilometers (248,800 square miles).

POPULATION (est. 1990): 2,423,200 people. _Density:_ 4 people per square kilometer.
10 people per square mile.
75% urban (city) living and 25% rural (country) living.

LARGEST CITY: (est. 1990) Edmonton - 785,000 people.

ELEVATION: _Highest:_ Mount Columbia - 3,747 meters (12,294 feet) above sea level.
Lowest: 170 meters (557 feet) above sea level along the Slave River.

ADDITIONAL INFORMATION: Alberta is one of the greatest oil-producing regions in all of North America. • Over four-fifths of Canada's natural gas comes from Alberta. • The province's standard of living is one of the highest in all of Canada. • Clear skies usually give Alberta more hours of sunshine throughout the year than any other province in Canada. • Alberta has long, cold winters and short, warm summers. • The North-West Mounted Police came to Alberta in 1874. The _Mounties_ drove liquor traders and outlaws from the region. • In 1954, for the first time, the combined value of Alberta mining and manufacturing became greater than that of agriculture.

Alberta's Flag

Flag Description

1. The background of the flag is blue.
2. The coat of arms is in the center of the flag. The cross is red on a white background and symbolizes the historic association with Great Britain.
3. The mountains and hills represent the Canadian Rockies. The wheat is Alberta's chief crop.
4. Color the flag the correct colors.

ALBERTA
"Sunny Alberta"

Name _____

Date _____

EARLY HISTORY in BRIEF

Before any white Europeans arrived in the region of today's Alberta, several Native American Indian tribes were living in the area. The Blackfoot Indian nation lived in the southern **prairies** and foothills. This great Indian nation included the Blackfoot, Blood, and Piegan tribes. **Allies** of the Blackfoot and the Sarcee also lived in the South. The Cree Indians roamed the northern forests. The Beaver, Gros Ventre and Stonies also lived throughout the Alberta region.

In 1670, King Charles II of England gave fur-trading rights to the Hudson's Bay Company. The region was part of a vast territory called *Rupert's Land*. In 1754, the first known white person to visit the region of Alberta was Anthony Henday. He was sent to the area by the Hudson's Bay Company in hopes of **promoting** trade with the Blackfoot Indians. He lived with the Blackfoot for a year, returning to York Factory in 1755.

An American named Peter Pond built a fur-trading post near Lake Athabasca in 1778. It was during the 1780's that a Montreal fur-trading company established the North West Company in the Alberta region. Hudson's Bay Company and the North West Company **competed** for the fur-trading business until 1821, when they **merged** their efforts.

In 1788, Roderick Mackenzie, a fur trader, established Fort Chipewyan. His cousin, Sir Alexander Mackenzie, traveled from the fort to the Arctic Ocean in 1789. Alexander then went to the Pacific Ocean in 1792-1793. From 1789 to 1812, David Thompson, a famous **geographer**, made **surveys** that provided the first good map of the Canadian Northwest.

During the mid-1800's, most of the settlers in the Alberta region were traders and people of mixed Indian and white **descent**. In 1840, a Methodist **missionary** named Robert T. Rundle was the first missionary in the region.

In 1870, the Hudson's Bay Company gave up Rupert's Land to the newly formed *Dominion of Canada*. The dominion paid the company $1.5 million and permitted the company to keep large areas of the **plains**. That same year, Canada established the North West Territories, which included the region of Alberta and the rest of the former Rupert's Land.

During this time, traders from Montana were illegally trading liquor with the Indians of the North West Territories. In order to stop this trade, the Canadian government created the North-West Mounted Police — called *Mounties*. The Mounties established their first post in the Alberta region in 1874. This post was built at Fort Macleod. The Mounties stopped the illegal liquor trades.

ALBERTA

Name _____

Date _____

The Mounties won the confidence and trust of the Indians living in the region. Within a few years, the Indians began giving up their land and moving to reservations. Only about 500 white settlers were living in the Alberta region in 1883. Most of these settlers were cattle rangers.

The grazing lands of the Alberta region drew thousands of farmers from eastern Canada, the United States, and northern and central Europe. In 1905, the Canadian government established the province of Alberta. Alexander Rutherford became its first **premier**. Alberta's first major oil discovery was made in the Turner Valley in 1914.

The province's name dates back to 1882. At that time, the Canadian government divided the region between British Columbia and Manitoba into four territory districts — Alberta, Assiniboia, Athabaska, and Saskatchewan. The Alberta district was named for Princess Louise Caroline Alberta, a daughter of Queen Victoria. The princess was also the wife of the Canadian governor general. The princess' first name was given to what is now Alberta's most famous lake in Banff National Park.

Among the duties of today's Royal Canadian Mounted Police, is to give advice and help tourists in Canada.

ALBERTA

Name _____

REVIEW QUESTIONS

Date _____

Circle the correct answer.

1. Who granted fur-trading rights to the Hudson's Bay Company?
    a. Rupert   b. The English   c. The French   d. King Charles II

2. In 1670, Alberta was part of the vast territory of ...
    a. Rupert's Land   b. Canada   c. New France   d. Peter's Pond

3. Alberta's first major oil discovery was in ...
    a. 1914   b. 1905   c. 1883   d. 1981

Fill in the blanks with the correct answer.

4. The _____ Indian nation lived in the _____ and _____ of the Alberta region.

5. The _____ Indians were _____ of the Blackfoot and also lived in the southern region.

6. The first Mounties' post in the region was built at _____.

7. Name the two companies that competed for the fur-trading business in the Alberta region: _____ _____

8. How much did Canada pay for Rupert's Land? _____.

9. Why did Peter Pond live with the Blackfoot for a year? _____
_____

10. Explain why the Mounties built a fort in the Alberta region.
_____
_____

Bonus ☆ ☆ ☆

Use another resource book and write a report on Peter Pond, Roderick Mackenzie, Canadian Mounted Police, Alexander Rutherford, Hudson's Bay Company, or the Blackfoot Indians. Include pictures and maps in your report if they are applicable.

CANADA: Section 3 - 20   © Golden Educational Center

BRITISH COLUMBIA

Map • Facts • History & Review Questions

New Words to Learn:
Find the words in a dictionary and write the meanings on the lines.

1. **annexation** - _____
2. **candidate** - _____
3. **colonization** - _____
4. **compromise** - _____
5. **controversy** - _____
6. **fiber** - _____
7. **fleet** - _____
8. **latitude** - _____
9. **Line of Demarcation** - _____
10. **parallel** - _____
11. **route** - _____
12. **totem pole** - _____

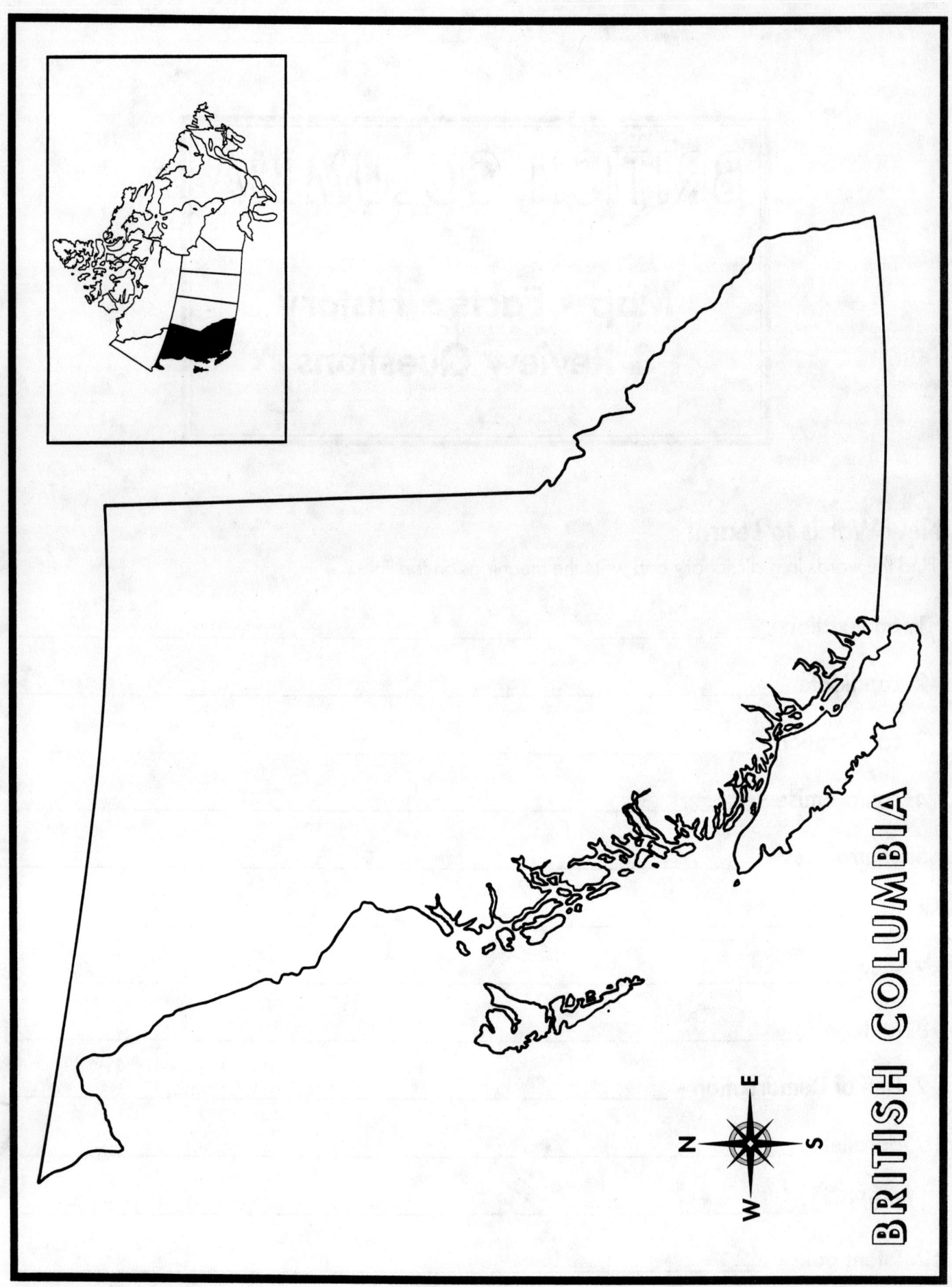

BRITISH COLUMBIA
(KOH-luhm-bee-uh)

Name _____

Date _____

BECAME A PROVINCE: July 20, 1871 — the 6th province.

CAPITAL CITY: Victoria.

AREA: 929,728 square kilometers (358,971 square miles).

POPULATION (est. 1990): 3,044,200 people.   <u>Density</u>: 3 people per square kilometer.
8 people per square mile.
77% urban (city) living and 23% rural (country) living.

LARGEST CITY: Vancouver - 1,380,000 people.

ELEVATION: <u>Highest</u>: Mount Fairweather - 4,663 meters (15,300 feet) above sea level.
<u>Lowest</u>: Sea level along the coast.

ADDITIONAL INFORMATION: British Columbia is Canada's third largest province according to size. Only Ontario and Quebec are larger. The province includes the Queen Charlotte Islands and Vancouver Island. British Columbia has a larger area than California, Oregon and Washington states combined. • More than half of the province's population lives in the Victoria-Vancouver (city) region in the southwestern corner of the province. • Trees from British Columbia provide about two-thirds of Canada's lumber. • Even today, people are building towns in several areas that had been almost totally unsettled.

British Columbia's Flag

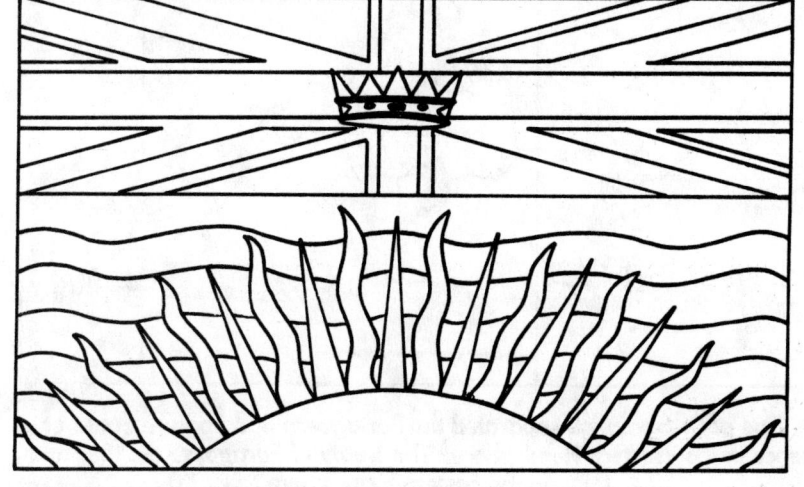

Flag Description

1. The gold crown in the middle of the Union Jack on the top half of the flag shows the association with Great Britain.

2. The setting sun is yellow and shows that British Columbia is the western most province in Canada.

3. Behind the sun are seven stripes. They alternate blue and white with white on the top and bottom stripes.

4. Color the flag the correct colors.

BRITISH COLUMBIA

"Beautiful British Columbia"

Name _____

Date _____

EARLY HISTORY in BRIEF

In 1774, a Spanish **fleet** of ships under the command of Juan Pérez sighted the region that is now British Columbia. However, they did not land.

Long before these Spanish sailors arrived into the area, Native American Indians were living in British Columbia. The two largest tribes were the Athabaskans in the north and the Salish in the Southern interior. The Haida, Kwakiutl, Nootka and Tsimshian tribes were the richest and most advanced. These tribes lived along the coast. They caught whales, sea otters, salmon and halibut for food. All of these tribes carved great **totem poles** out of trees.

The Indians living in the interior traveled along the larger rivers and hunted and fished for their food. They dug *keek-wilie houses* in the ground for winter shelter. The roofs of these houses were made of wood and then covered with soil. During the summer, these Indians built *mat lodges* to live in. These mat houses were made of wood frames and covered with **fiber** mats or branches.

James Cook was the first white man to actually land in the British Columbia region. He led two British ships into Nootka Sound on the west coast of Vancouver Island in 1778. He was searching for a passage from the Pacific Ocean to the Atlantic Ocean. His men traded trinkets to the Indians for otter skins, and later sold the skins in China. By 1786, the British had built a very profitable fur trade business with the Indians in the region.

By 1789, the Nootka Sound **Controversy** had developed. Spain had claimed the area because of Pérez' voyage, and because treaties between Spain and Portugal gave all the land west of the **Line of Demarcation** (established in 1493) to Spain. The Spanish became concerned about the growing British trade in the region. They seized control of several British ships in Nootka Sound. The two countries almost went to war over the dispute, but they resolved their differences in 1790. However, ownership of the area remained unsettled.

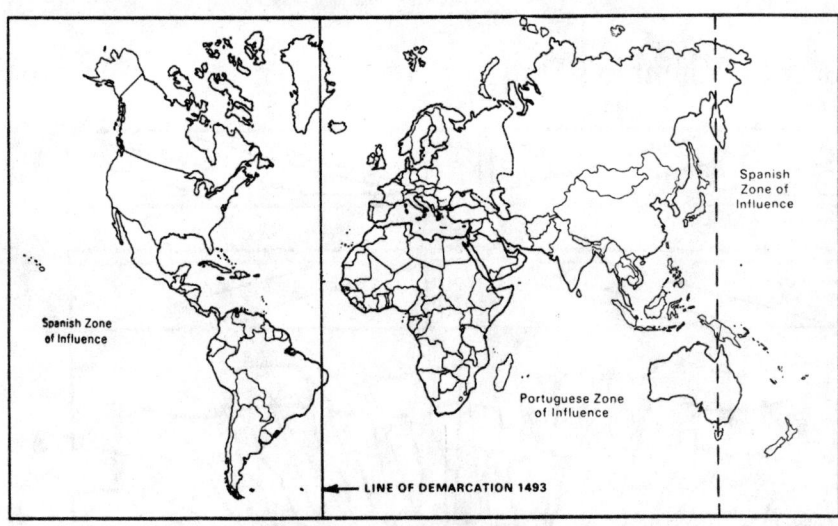

The *Line of Demarcation* separated the Portuguese and Spanish zones of influence in the Western Hemisphere. The *Treaty of Saragossa* did the same thing in the Eastern Hemisphere.

BRITISH COLUMBIA

Name _____

Date _____

    The English explorer, George Vancouver, began his three-year voyage to survey the Pacific Coast from Oregon to Alaska. On this voyage, he and his men named many of the inlets and coastal features.

    In 1793, Alexander Mackenzie, a Scottish fur trader from eastern Canada, crossed the Rocky Mountains and reached the Pacific Ocean. Two other fur traders were sent to the region by the North West Company. One was Simon Fraser who came in 1805. David Thompson was another man who came to the region in 1807. Both men opened fur-trading posts as they came west from eastern Canada. Their chain of posts became Canada's overland fur-trade **route**. In 1808, Fraser explored the river which now has his name. Thompson reached the mouth of the Columbia River in 1811.

    The Hudson's Bay Company was a very powerful British trading business. The company controlled the fur-trade in British Columbia as well as the area of present-day Washington and Oregon — before they were territories of the United States. During the late 1830's and early 1840's, many American settlers moved into the southern part of this region. They ignored the authority of the British company, and asked the United States to establish a government in the area.

    Democratic presidential **candidates** of the United States made claims to the territory as an issue in the 1844 presidential election campaign. They wanted the United States to have the territory on the Pacific Coast as far north as **latitude** 54°40'. The British wanted the southern border of British Columbia to follow the 49th **parallel** from the Rocky Mountains to the Columbia River, and then follow the river south and west. This would have made British Columbia to include all of today's western Washington. James Polk, a Democrat, won the presidential election. He offered a **compromise** that set the British territory's southern boundary at the 49th parallel except for Vancouver Island. The British kept all of Vancouver Island even though part of it lies below the 49th parallel. The United States and Great Britain signed a treaty establishing the two borders in 1846.

    The Hudson's Bay Company founded Fort Victoria (now Victoria) in 1843. The British government gave the company the entire island for **colonization** in 1849. It became the British colony of Vancouver Island. The British wanted to strengthen their claims to the mainland region, so they formed the Colony of British Columbia in 1858. The colony's capital was established at New Westminster. In order to cut governmental costs, the British united the two colonies in 1866. New Westminster was the capital until 1868, when Victoria became the capital.

    Colonists argued whether they should apply for **annexation** to the United States, or become a province in the new Dominion of Canada. In 1871, they agreed to become part of Canada, on the condition the Canadian government build a railroad to link eastern Canada to British Columbia. It took ten years for the government to begin construction of the railroad.

BRITISH COLUMBIA

Name _____

REVIEW QUESTIONS

Date _____

Fill in the blanks with the correct answer.

1. British Columbia's largest city according to population is _____.

2. In 1846, the Great Britain and the _____ signed a _____ establishing the two borders. The boundary was established at the _____ instead of following the Columbia River.

3. British Columbia is the _____ largest province in Canada.

4. In what area does most of the population live? _____

5. What was the year British Columbia become a colony? _____

6. Why did Great Britain establish the colony? _____
_____

7. Explain why Vancouver Island is part of Canada, yet lies partly below the 49th parallel.
_____
_____
_____
_____

8. What is the Line of Demarcation? _____
_____
_____

9. Explain why British Columbia became part of Canada instead of the United States.
_____
_____

Bonus ☆ ☆ ☆
Use another resource book and write a report on totem poles, Alexander Mackenzie, Simon Fraser, the Columbia River, Rocky Mountains, James Polk, or one of the Indian tribes mentioned in history. Include pictures and maps in your report if they are applicable.

MANITOBA

Map • Facts • History & Review Questions

New Words to Learn:
Find the words in a dictionary and write the meanings on the lines.

1. **caribou** - _____

2. **dispute** - _____

3. **expedition** - _____

4. **game** - _____

5. **keystone** - _____

6. **livestock** - _____

7. **prosper** - _____

8. **wanderer** - _____

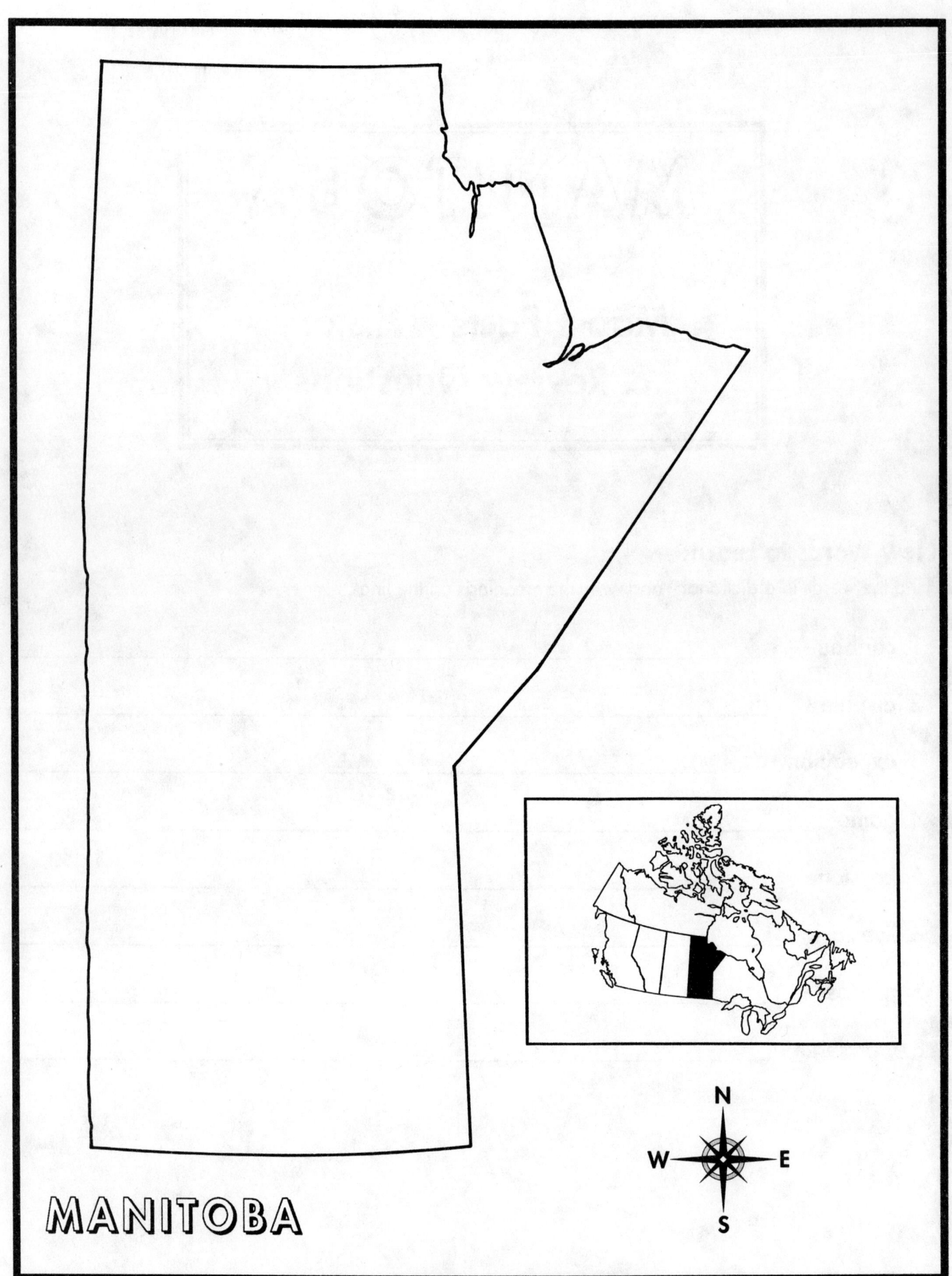

MANITOBA
(man–uh–TOH–buh)

Name _____

Date _____

BECAME A PROVINCE: July 15, 1870 — the 5th province.

CAPITAL CITY: Winnipeg.

AREA: 548,360 square kilometers   (211,723 square miles)

POPULATION (est. 1990): 1,083,300 people.   <u>Density</u>: 2 people per square kilometer.
5 people per square mile.
70% urban (city) living and 30% rural (country) living.

LARGEST CITY: Winnipeg - 625,000 people.

ELEVATION: <u>Highest</u>: Baldy Mountain - 832 meters (2,729 feet) above sea level.
<u>Lowest</u>: Sea level along Hudson Bay.

ADDITIONAL INFORMATION: Manitoba is one of Canada's three Prairie Provinces. • It lies halfway between the Pacific and Atlantic Oceans. • Almost half of Manitoba's population lives in Winnipeg. • St. Boniface has the largest cattle stockyard in all of Canada. • Manitoba ranks among the leading North American producers of zinc and nickel. • The province is famous for the high quality of wheat and grain it produces. • Manitoba has the nickname of the *Keystone Province*. The nickname came from the location of the province being in the center, or **keystone**, of the "arch" formed by the ten Canadian provinces.

Manitoba's Flag

Flag Description

1. The background of the flag is red.
2. The coat of arms is on the right. The buffalo symbolizes it's importance in Manitoba's history and the position of Manitoba as a Prairie Province.
3. The British Union Jack is in the upper right corner. The cross at the top of the coat of arms is red on a white background. Both represent the bond with Britain.
4. Color the flag the correct colors.

© GOLDEN EDUCATIONAL CENTER

CANADA: **Section 5 - 29**

MANITOBA
"Keystone Province"

Name _____

Date _____

EARLY HISTORY in BRIEF

When the first white explorers and fur traders arrived in the region of today's Manitoba, there were five main Indian tribes living in the region. The Chipewyan Indians lived in the northern section of the region. They hunted **caribou** to eat. The Woods Cree Indians were **wanderers** who hunted for moose and beaver. They lived in the central forest region. The Plains Cree fished and trapped animals in the prairies and wooded lowlands. The Assiniboin Indians lived on the southwestern plains and hunted buffalo. The Chippewa lived in the southeastern part of the plains and also hunted buffalo.

The first known white man to reach the region of Manitoba was the English explorer, Sir Thomas Button. He sailed down the west coast of Hudson Bay in 1612. He spent the winter at the mouth of the Nelson River, and claimed the surrounding area for England.

In 1670, King Charles II of England, granted trading rights to the Hudson's Bay Company of London. This entire region was called *Rupert's Land*. By 1690, French-Canadian fur traders were moving westward into the company's territory. The English company and French-Canadians fought many battles over fur-trading and territorial **disputes**. The Hudson's Bay Company sent Henry Kelsey on an **expedition** to find new sources of fur. From 1690 to 1692, Kelsey traveled among the Indians living in central and southern Manitoba. Many of the Indians he contacted began trading with the company.

It was in 1731 that Pierre Gaultier de Varennes, Sieur da la Vérendryen, left Montreal in search for an overland to the Pacific Ocean. He and his men were French-Canadian fur traders. They built several forts between Lake Superior and the Lower Saskatchewan River. One of these forts was Fort Rouge — built in 1738. It was built where present-day Winnipeg is located. His efforts in establishing fur trade in the region cut into the trade of the Hudson's Bay Company.

France was defeated by the British in the French and Indian War in 1763. As a result, France had to give Britain all of its land holdings in Canada. France also stopped all of its exploration and trade in the Manitoba region.

In 1783, the North West Company was established in the town of Montreal in order to compete with the Hudson's Bay Company. This competition for the fur trade business forced the Hudson's Bay Company to build posts to defend its trade.

MANITOBA

Name _____

Date _____

    While the two fur trading companies were competing for trade, the first farming settlement in the Manitoba region was being established. In 1811, Sir Thomas Douglas received a land grant from the Hudson's Bay Company. It included an area of more than 260,000 square kilometers (100,000 square miles) along the Red River. Thomas sent several groups of Scottish Highlanders and Irishmen to the area. These first farming settlers arrived in 1812.

    These early colonists suffered many hardships. At first, they had to hunt buffalo and other **game** animals in order to live. Farm equipment, **livestock**, and other supplies were brought into the area from the United States. With the equipment, hard work and good fortune with the weather, the production of goods gradually increased.

    As the Red River colony **prospered**, it expanded and eventually interfered with the fur trade of the North West Company. The company turned its trappers against the settlers. The trappers tried to force the farmers out of the region by burning their homes and destroying their crops. The fighting reached its peak in 1816. Peace was not totally restored to the region until 1821, when the North West Company combined with the Hudson's Bay Company.

    The Dominion of Canada was created in 1867. Almost immediately, it tried to acquire Rupert's Land, which included the Manitoba region, from the Hudson's Bay Company. The British government pressured the company to give up its rights to almost all of Rupert's Land. In 1869, the company agreed to give up its rights for $1,500,000. Great Britain then made plans to unite Rupert's Land with Canada.

    The métis in Manitoba opposed the union with Canada because they were afraid that settlers would move into the area and take their land. While using buffalo hunters as soldiers, they captured Fort Garry, present-day Winnipeg, and set up their own government. In 1870, the Canadian government granted the métis a bill of rights in *The Manitoba Act*. This act made Manitoba the fifth province of Canada.

    The word *Manitoba* probably came from the Algonkian language of the Indians. The tribes thought the *manito — great spirit —* made the echoing sounds that came from a **strait** of Lake Manitoba. The sounds were actually made by waves hitting against the shore. The Indians called this narrow part of the lake *Manito waba — great spirit's strait.* ❑

In July, people from far away places come together at a reconstructed Mennonite town to share in dancing, singing and food from their different cultures. Russians were the first to settle in that area in 1874.

© GOLDEN EDUCATIONAL CENTER

CANADA: Section 5 – 31

MANITOBA

Name _____

REVIEW QUESTIONS   Date _____

Circle the correct answer.

1. Who was the first white man to reach the region of Manitoba?
   a. Sir Button   b. A. Hudson   c. R. Nelson   d. Sieur Vérendryen

2. When did Manitoba become a province?
   a. 1783   b. 1867   c. 1869   d. 1870

3. When was the North West Company formed?
   a. 1783   b. 1867   c. 1869   d. 1870

Fill in the blanks with the correct answer.

4. The capital city of Manitoba is _____ . According to _____ it is also Manitoba's _____ city.

5. _____ was sent to Manitoba by the _____ _____ to find new sources of _____ .

6. List the five Indians tribes who lived in the Manitoba region before any white people arrived.

   _____   _____
   _____   _____
             _____

7. What is Manitoba famous for? _____

8. Explain why Manitoba's nickname is *Keystone Province*.

   _____
   _____
   _____

Bonus ☆ ☆ ☆

Use another resource book and write a report on one of the Indian tribes mentioned in history, cattle raising, Sir Thomas Button, the Manitoba Act, Rupert's Land, or Henry Kelsey. Include pictures and maps in your report if they are applicable.

NEW BRUNSWICK

Map • Facts • History & Review Questions

New Words to Learn:
Find the words in a dictionary and write the meanings on the lines.

1. **arable** - _____

2. **decline** - _____

3. **enforce** - _____

4. **execute** - _____

5. **expansion** - _____

6. **grant** - _____

7. **incorporate** - _____

8. **industry** - _____

9. **rivalry** - _____

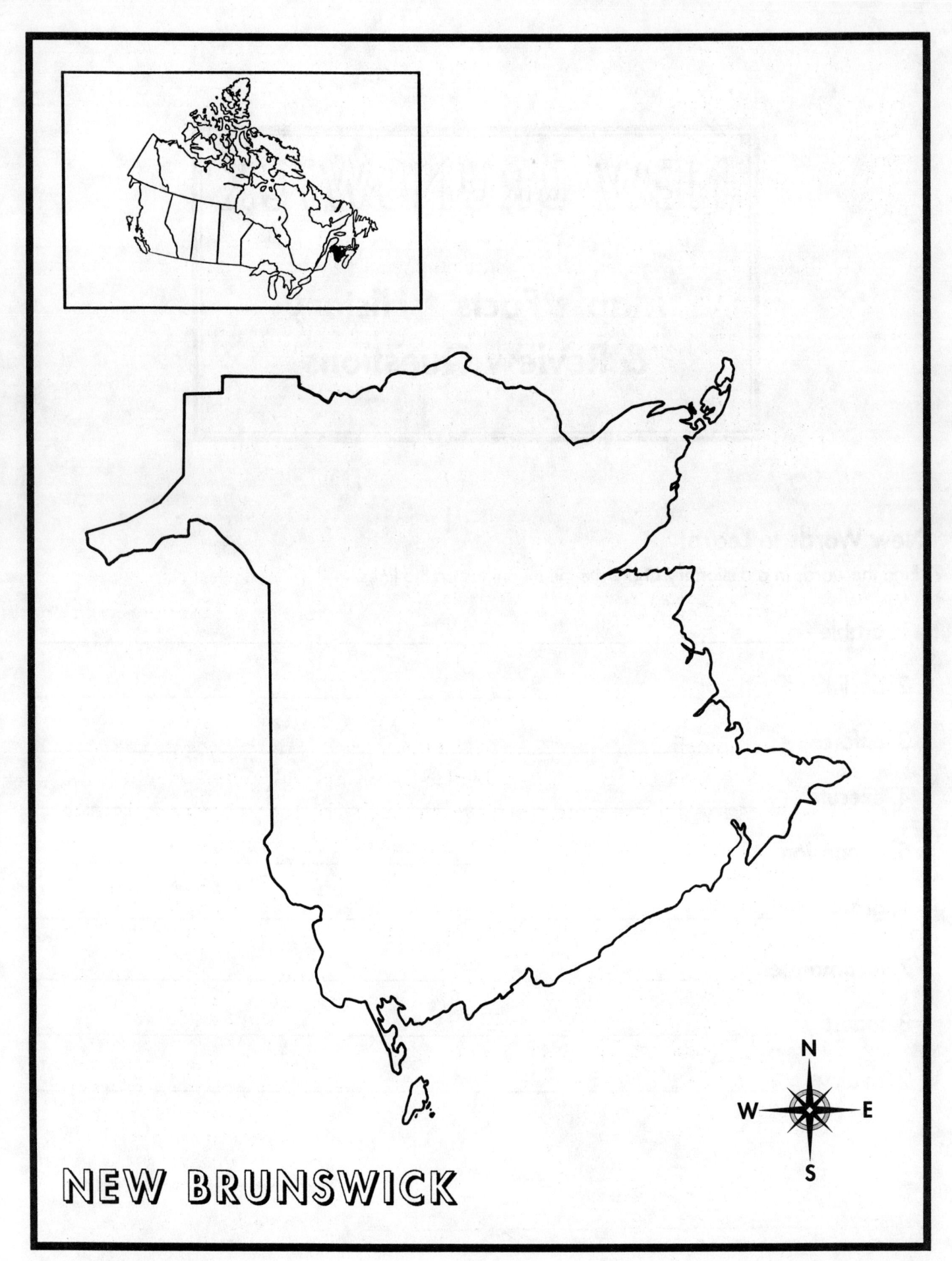

NEW BRUNSWICK

CANADA: Section 6 - 34

© Golden Educational Center

NEW BRUNSWICK
(NOO BRUHNS–wik)

Name _____

Date _____

BECAME A PROVINCE: July 1, 1867 — one of the four original provinces.

CAPITAL CITY: Fredericton.

AREA: 72,090 square kilometers   (27,834 square miles).

POPULATION (est. 1990): 717,600 people.   <u>Density</u>: 10 people per square kilometer.
26 people per square mile.
52% urban (city) living and 48% rural (country) living.

LARGEST CITY: Saint John - 76,400 people.

ELEVATION: <u>Highest</u>: Mount Carleton - 820 meters (2,690 feet) above sea level.
<u>Lowest</u>: Sea level along the coast.

ADDITIONAL INFORMATION: New Brunswick is one of the four Atlantic Provinces of Canada. • Ninety percent of the land is covered by forests. • Paper and pulp mills use wood from the forests to produce newsprint — papers used in printing newspapers and other paper products. • New Brunswick is in the midst of an **industrial expansion.** • The province was named for the British royal family of Brunswick-Lüneburg — the House of Hanover. Most of its early settlers were American colonists who remained loyal to Britain during the American Revolutionary War. As a result of these United Empire Loyalists moving into the region, New Brunswick received the nickname of the *Loyalist Province*.

New Brunswick's Flag

Flag Description

1. The lion on the top of the flag is gold on a red background. It represents the tie with Great Britain.

2. The ship represents New Brunswick's early shipbuilding industry. The ship is black with a white mainsail and red flags on the masts. The background is gold. The stripes at the bottom, showing water, alternate blue and white with blue on the top and bottom.

3. Color the flag the correct colors.

NEW BRUNSWICK

"Loyalist Province" & "Picture Province"

Name _____

Date _____

EARLY HISTORY in BRIEF

When the first white settlers came to the region of New Brunswick in the early 1600's, they found the Micmac and Maliseet (also called the Malecite) Indians living in the area. Both of these tribes belonged to the Algonkian Indian family. The Micmac lived in the eastern part of the region, while the Maliseet lived in the St. John River Valley.

The Indians learned that the best fishing areas were usually downstream from waterfalls in rivers. They camped near the fishing spots where they caught salmon and trout. Indians who lived along the coast caught porpoises and gathered clams and oysters for food. Only a few Indian groups farmed for their food. They mostly grew corn and pumpkins.

In 1534, the French explorer, Jacques Cartier sailed into Chaleur Bay. He wrote the following quote as he described the countryside of the New Brunswick region:

> "The land along the south side of it is as fine and as good land, as **arable** and as full of beautiful fields and meadows, as any we have ever seen..."

It wasn't until 1604, that any further exploration took place in the New Brunswick region. That year, the French explorer, Samuel de Champlain and Pierre du Guast, Sieur de Monts, sailed into the Bay of Fundy. After they explored the coast, they established a settlement on St. Croix Island — near the mouth of the St. Croix River. A year later, the settlement was moved across the bay to Port Royal, in what is now Nova Scotia. French fur trappers and traders continued to move into the region throughout the 1600's. They called the region *Acadia*.

The French continually fought each other for control over the valuable fur-trading business. The most famous of the battles was between Charles de la Tour and D'Aulnay de Charnisay. La Tour had a fort and post where Saint John sits today. In 1645, while La Tour was absent from his fort, de Charnisay attacked it. Marie de la Tour, Charles' wife, led the defense. However, she and her men finally had to surrender. De Charnisay forced her to watch all of her men be hanged, except the one who was forced to be the **executioner**.

As the **rivalry** between the French and the British grew, the competition among the French fur traders gradually **declined**. To the south (today's United States), British colonies were growing rapidly. Many British fur traders and fishermen moved into the New Brunswick region from the south.

NEW BRUNSWICK

Name _____

Date _____

The British conquered Acadia twice during the late 1600's. They returned it both times to France. In 1713, after the Queen Anne's War, France gave Acadia to England in the *Peace of Utrecht*. However, the Acadians did not move from the New Brunswick region. With England being across the Atlantic Ocean, it was almost impossible to **enforce** the new ownership. During the last part of the French and Indian Wars, British troops captured the region. They succeeded in driving out most of the Acadians. The *Treaty of Paris in 1763*, confirmed England's ownership of Acadia.

Traders from New England settled in Saint John in 1762. A year later, other New Englanders established the settlement of Maugerville — near today's Fredericton. That same year, the New Brunswick region became a part of the British province of Nova Scotia. Many of the Acadians that were driven from their homes by the British troops were allowed to return. They received **grants** of land in the North and East.

In 1783, after the American Revolutionary War, about 14,000 people loyal to England moved to the New Brunswick region from the United States. Most of them settled in the lower St. John River Valley. They founded the settlement of Fredericton. In 1784, Great Britain established New Brunswick as a separate province. In 1785, Saint John became the first **incorporated** city in what is now Canada.

Samuel de Champlain explored Canada's east coast and founded Quebec, the first city, in 1608.

Lord Durham urged Great Briatin to give Canadian colonies self government in 1839.

© GOLDEN EDUCATIONAL CENTER

CANADA: Section 6 – 37

NEW BRUNSWICK

Name _____

REVIEW QUESTIONS

Date _____

Circle the correct answer.

1. What percent of the countryside is covered with forests?
   a. 10%   b. 50%   c. 75%   d. 90%

2. What year did New Brunswick become a province?
   a. 1783   b. 1870   c. 1869   d. 1867

3. Most of the first white people came to New Brunswick from which country?
   a. France   b. England   c. Great Britain   d. United States

Fill in the blanks with the correct answer.

4. The capital city of New Brunswick is _____ .

5. What year did the first European explorer arrive in the New Brunswick region? _____ How long was it until the next exploration took place in the region? _____

6. What did the French fur traders call the New Brunswick region? _____

7. Saint John became what? _____

8. Explain why New Brunswick is sometimes called the *Loyalist Province*.
   _____
   _____
   _____
   _____
   _____
   _____
   _____

Bonus ☆ ☆ ☆

Use another resource book and write a report on Loyalists, Jacques Cartier, paper manufacturing, porpoises, American Revolutionary War, Acadians, or Charles de la Tour. Include pictures and maps in your report if they are applicable.

NEWFOUNDLAND

Map • Facts • History & Review Questions

New Words to Learn:
Find the words in a dictionary and write the meanings on the lines.

1. **archaeology** - _____
2. **commission** - _____
3. **community** - _____
4. **hemisphere** - _____
5. **income** - _____
6. **mineral** - _____
7. **noble** - _____
8. **suspend** - _____

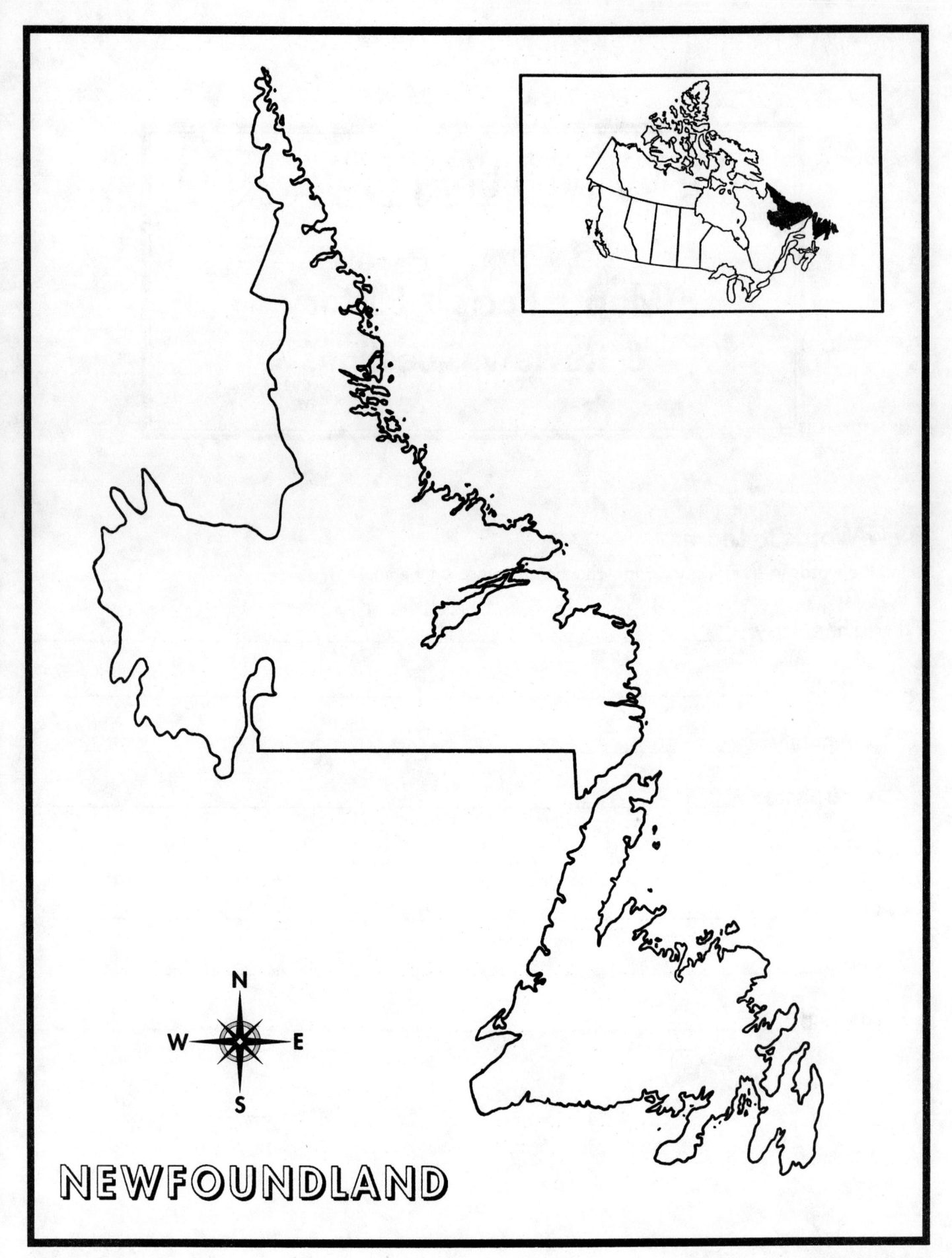

NEWFOUNDLAND

CANADA: Section 7 - 40

© Golden Educational Center

NEWFOUNDLAND
(noo–fun–LAND)

Name _____

Date _____

BECAME A PROVINCE: March 31, 1949 — the 10th province.

CAPITAL CITY: St. John's.

AREA: 371,689 square kilometers (143,510 square miles).

POPULATION (est. 1990): 529,200 people.   <u>Density</u>: 1 person per square kilometer.
4 people per square mile.
57% urban (city) living and 43% rural (country) living.

LARGEST CITY: St. John's - 96,200 people.

ELEVATION: <u>Highest</u>: Mont d'Iberville - 1,646 meters (5,400 feet) above sea level.
<u>Lowest</u>: Sea level.

ADDITIONAL INFORMATION: Newfoundland is Canada's newest province. The province includes the island of Newfoundland and the coast of Labrador, a part of mainland Canada. • St. John's is one of the oldest **communities** in all of North America. Newfoundland has a longer history than any other English speaking region in all of North America. • Of all of the Canadian provinces, only Prince Edward Island has fewer people than Newfoundland. Almost all of the people live near the sea. • Some fishing fleets travel halfway around the world to fish in the area called *Grand Banks*, southeast of Newfoundland. • Mining is Newfoundland's main source of **income**.

Newfoundland's Flag

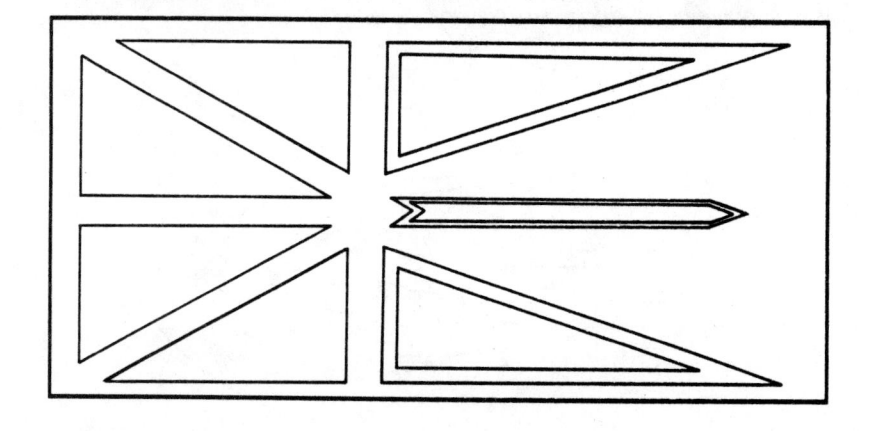

Flag Description

1. The background of the flag is white.
2. The four triangles on the left are blue.
3. The two triangles on the right are red outlines with white centers.
4. The arrow is outlined in red with a yellow center.
5. Color the flag the correct colors.

NEWFOUNDLAND
"Britain's Oldest Colony"

Name _____

Date _____

EARLY HISTORY in BRIEF

Vikings were most likely the first Europeans to live in the region of Newfoundland. In 1961, **archaeologists** discovered the ruins of a Viking settlement on the northern tip of the island. These scientists believe this settlement could have been built as early as A.D. 1000. The Vikings arrived on the Western **Hemisphere** almost 500 years before the famed Christopher Columbus. English fishermen also reached the coast of Newfoundland before Columbus. These fishermen from Bristol probably arrived in 1481. John Cabot, the Italian explorer hired by England, might have landed in Newfoundland or Nova Scotia in 1497. Cabot thought he had reached Asia. He realized that Newfoundland had rich fishing grounds and took the news back to Europe.

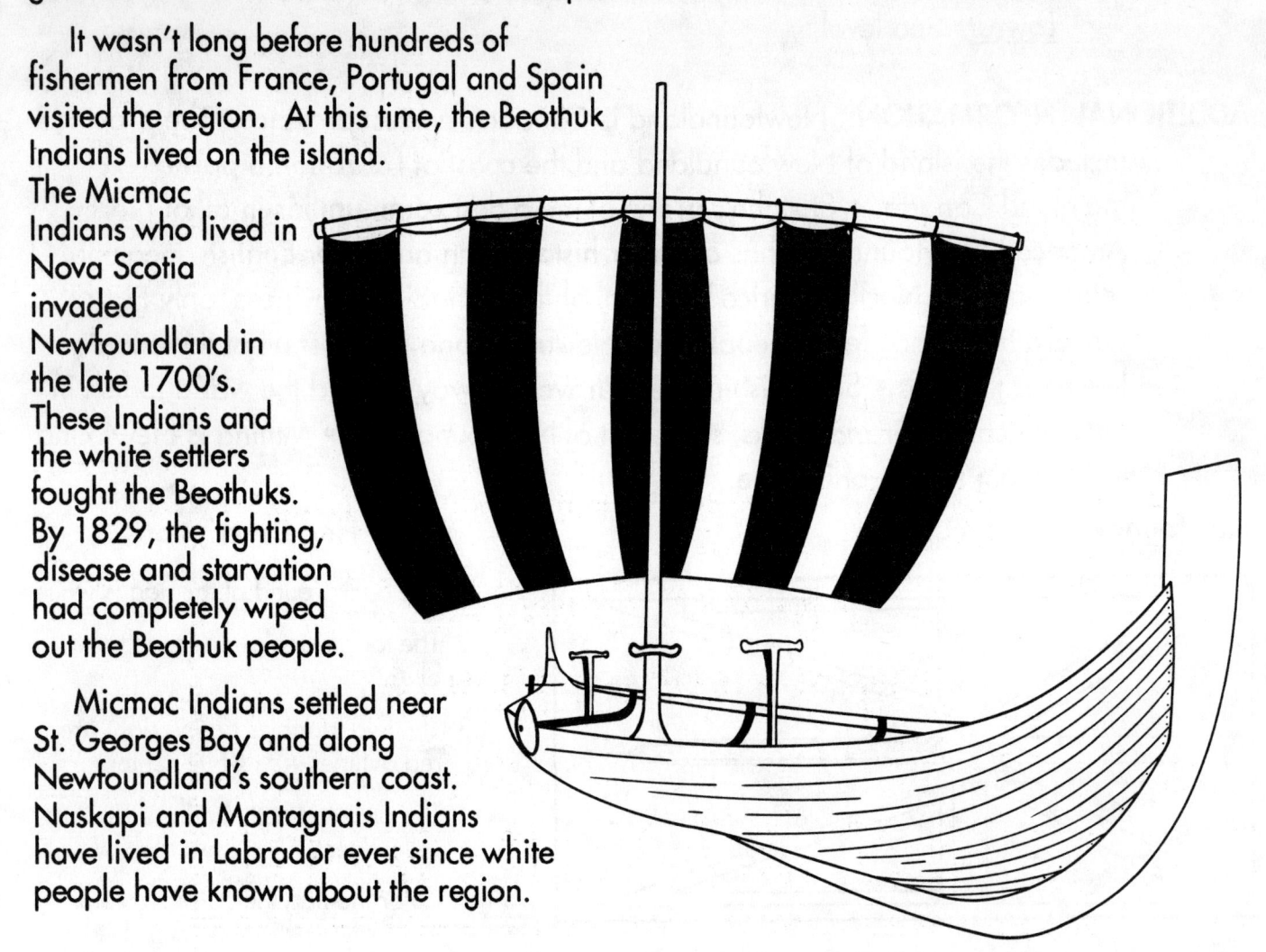

It wasn't long before hundreds of fishermen from France, Portugal and Spain visited the region. At this time, the Beothuk Indians lived on the island. The Micmac Indians who lived in Nova Scotia invaded Newfoundland in the late 1700's. These Indians and the white settlers fought the Beothuks. By 1829, the fighting, disease and starvation had completely wiped out the Beothuk people.

Micmac Indians settled near St. Georges Bay and along Newfoundland's southern coast. Naskapi and Montagnais Indians have lived in Labrador ever since white people have known about the region.

This ship is believed to have been the same kind used to cross the Atlantic Ocean by Vikings.

CANADA: Section 7 - 42

© GOLDEN EDUCATIONAL CENTER

NEWFOUNDLAND

Name _____

Date _____

By the late 1500's, fishermen from several different European countries had established settlements on Newfoundland. The English fishermen settled and fished mainly along the southern part of the east coast. French fishermen mostly controlled the north and south coasts. However, it was common to see English, French, Spanish and Portuguese ships anchored in the same bay or harbor.

In 1583, the English explorer, Sir Humphrey Gilbert landed at St. John's harbor. He claimed "200 leagues" (about 970 kilometers, or 600 miles) in every direction for England. In 1637, King Charles I granted Newfoundland to Sir David Kirke and other **nobles**. Kirke set up his headquarters at Ferryland. However, he had no authority over the fishermen who came to the island each summer. Kirke returned to England in 1651, at the request of the English government.

French settlers founded Placentia in 1662. The new French settlement grew rapidly and threatened England's control of Newfoundland. In 1689, William III, the king of England, declared war on France. Newfoundland became a battleground for the war. English and French ships attacked one another until 1713, when the two counties signed the *Treaty of Utrecht*. The treaty gave Britain control of the entire island. However, France got to use part of the northwestern shore for drying fish. That area became known as the *French Shore*. During the Seven Years' War (1756-1763), English fishermen drove the French fishermen from the French Shore. By the *Treaty of Paris in 1763*, Great Britain gained control of all of Canada. In return, France received Saint Pierre and Miquelon islands from Britain. France also gained the right to use the French Shore. In 1904, France gave up this right.

Shortly after the signing of the treaty, the British placed the Labrador coast under the authority of Newfoundland's governor. Newfoundland lost control of Labrador to Quebec in 1774, regained it in 1809, and then divided it with Quebec in 1825. (The present boundary between the coast of Labrador and Quebec was established in 1927. This boundary decision gave Newfoundland the vast **mineral** resources of the Knob Lake and Wabush Lake regions.)

In 1855, as an English colony, Newfoundland was allowed to set up its own government. In 1834, Britain **suspended** Newfoundland's government and established a **Commission** *of Government*. This government had a British governor and six other men, three of which were from Newfoundland. Newfoundland became a dependency of Great Britain, and Britain took over its debts.

In 1948, Newfoundland people voted to unite with Canada rather than keep the Commission of Government or return to independent self-government. On March 31, 1949, Newfoundland became Canada's tenth province.

NEWFOUNDLAND

Name _____

REVIEW QUESTIONS Date _____

Circle the correct answer.

1. What year did Newfoundland become a province?
   a. 1948   b. 1867   c. 1949   d. 1834

2. What year did Newfoundland become an English colony?
   a. 1948   b. 1855   c. 1949   d. 1834

3. Who were the first Europeans to visit the Newfoundland region?
   a. English   b. Vikings   c. French   d. Spanish

Fill in the blanks with the correct answer.

4. The capital city of Newfoundland is _____ .

5. What is an archaeologist? _____
_____

They have discovered that the first _____ to live in the Newfoundland region were most likely _____ . There is evidence that they settled in the area as early as _____ . The _____ arrived on the Western _____ almost 500 years before _____ .

6. What led to the destruction of the Beothuk Indians? _____
_____

7. What were the results of the *Treaty of Paris in 1763?*
_____
_____
_____
_____

Bonus ☆ ☆ ☆

Use another resource book and write a report on Green Banks, the Vikings, archaeology, commercial fishing, Portugal, Spain, Great Britain, John Cabot, or one of the Indian tribes mentioned in the history. Include pictures and maps in your report if they are applicable.

CANADA: Section 7 - 44   © GOLDEN EDUCATIONAL CENTER

NOVA SCOTIA

Map • Facts • History & Review Questions

New Words to Learn:
Find the words in a dictionary and write the meanings on the lines.

1. **allegiance** - _____

2. **continent** - _____

3. **migrate** - _____

4. **persecution** - _____

5. **Protestant** - _____

6. **swear** - _____

7. **tide** - _____

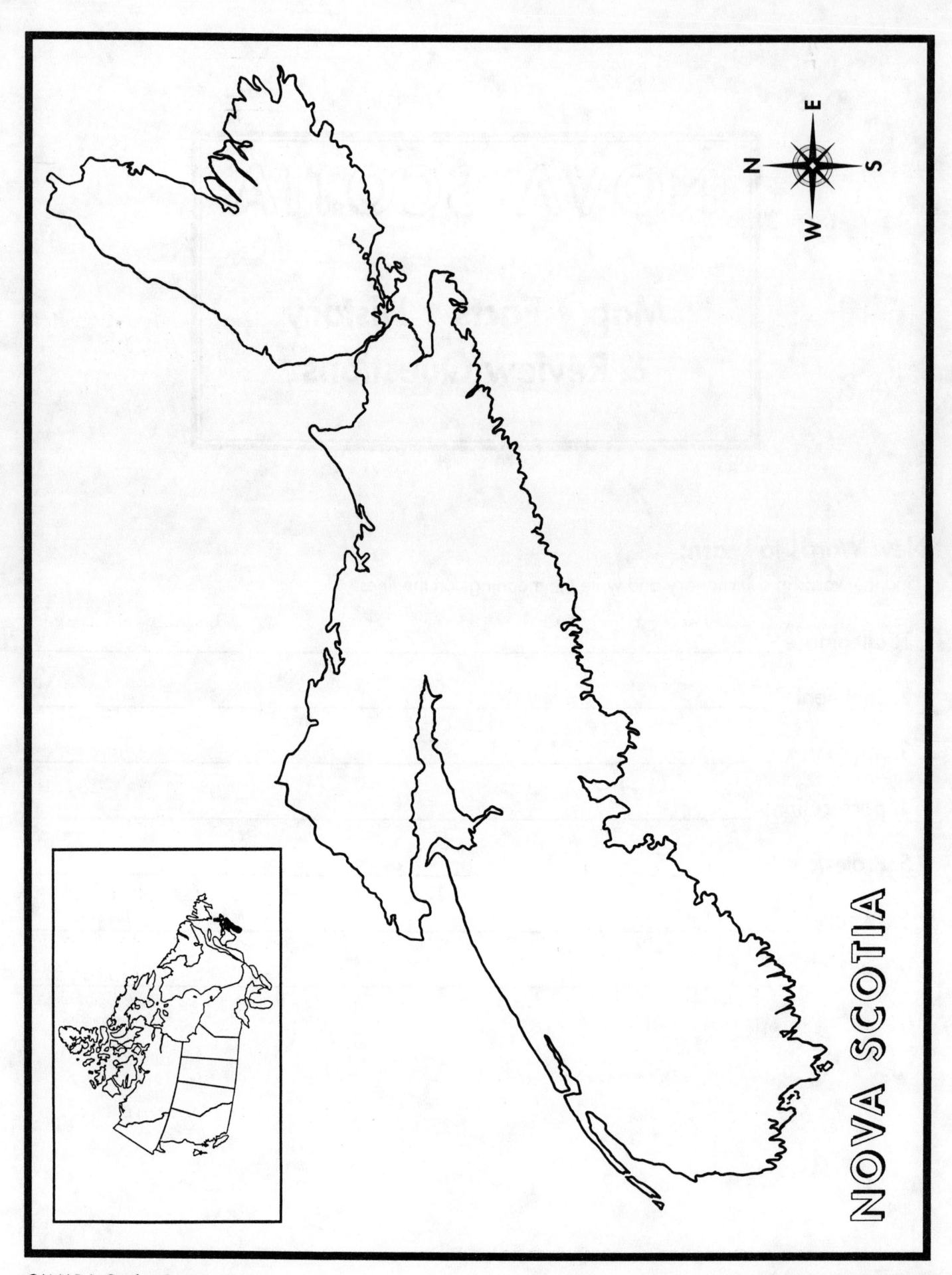

NOVA SCOTIA

CANADA: Section 8 - 46

NOVA SCOTIA
(NO-vuh SKO-shuh)

Name _____

Date _____

BECAME A PROVINCE: July 1, 1867 — one of the four original provinces.

CAPITAL CITY: Halifax.

AREA: 52,841 square kilometers (20,402 square miles).

POPULATION (est. 1990): 885,700 people.   <u>Density</u>: 17 people per square kilometer.
   43 people per square mile.
   56% urban (city) living and 44% rural (country) living.

LARGEST CITY: Halifax - 113,600 people.

ELEVATION: <u>Highest</u>: 532 meters (1,747 feet) above sea level in Cape Breton Highlands National Park.
   <u>Lowest</u>: Sea level along the coast.

ADDITIONAL INFORMATION: Nova Scotia is one of the four Atlantic Provinces of Canada.
• No part of the Province is more than 56 kilometers (35 miles) from the sea.
• Ocean **tides** sometimes rise higher in Nova Scotia than anywhere else in the world. Sometimes, they rise more than 15 meters (50 feet) at the bay of Fundy.
• Sable Island lies about 160 kilometers (100 miles) off the southern coast of Nova Scotia. It is formed entirely by sand. Sailors call the island the *Graveyard of the Atlantic* because it has caused so many shipwrecks over the years.

Nova Scotia's Flag

Flag Description

1. The flag is white with a blue cross.

2. The lion in the center is red on a gold background. It symbolizes the association of Nova Scotia with Scotland. (Nova Scotia means *New Scotland*).

3. Color the flag the correct colors.

© Golden Educational Center

NOVA SCOTIA
"Land of Evangeline"

Name _____

Date _____

EARLY HISTORY in BRIEF

The Micmac Indians were the first known settlers in the Nova Scotia region. They fished for their food along the coast in the summer, and hunted moose and caribou in the forests in the winter.

The explorer, John Cabot, probably landed on the coast of Nova Scotia or Newfoundland as early as 1497, only seven years after Christopher Columbus happened upon the **continent**. Cabot believed he had landed in Asia. From 1520 to 1525, several other explorers reached Nova Scotia while searching for a westward sea route to Asia.

During the late 1500's, French fishermen used the shore of Nova Scotia for drying the codfish they had caught in the nearby waters. They stayed to fish in the region during the Summers and returned to France in the Autumn.

In 1603, the king of France, King Henry IV, gave land which included Nova Scotia to a French explorer. His name was Pierre du Guast, Sieur de Monts. De Monts and another French explorer, Samuel de Champlain, explored the coast of Nova Scotia in 1604. Champlain made the first accurate map of the coast. The French called the Nova Scotia region and the land around it *Acadia*. De Monts and Champlain established a settlement in the New Brunswick region, and then moved it to Nova Scotia in 1605. This first settlement became Port Royal.

Eight years later, English men from Virginia captured and burned the French settlement at Port Royal. Off and on over the next hundred years, the French and English fought for control of Acadia.

In 1621, King James I of England and Scotland granted Acadia to Sir William Alexander. The grant included what is now Nova Scotia, as well as New Brunswick, Prince Edward Island, part of Quebec and part of Maine. Alexander renamed the entire region *Nova Scotia*, which is Latin for *New Scotland*.

Britain gave Port Royal to France in 1632, under the provisions of the *Treaty of St. Germain-en-Laye*. Settlers sent by a French company took control of Port Royal and La Havre. These settlers became known as *Acadians*. In 1636, the French built a new fort near Port Royal, on the present-day site of Annapolis Royal.

British troops captured Port Royal in 1690. However, Britain gave the settlement back to France under the Treaty of Ryswick in 1697. Troops from both England and New England fought together to recapture Port Royal again in 1710. That year, the British changed the name of the fort from Port Royal to Annapolis Royal.

CANADA: Section 8 - 48

© GOLDEN EDUCATIONAL CENTER

NOVA SCOTIA

Name _____

Date _____

France finally gave up all its claims to Nova Scotia under the *Peace of Utrecht in 1713*. This treaty put all of the French Acadians who remained in Nova Scotia under the authority of the British government. The treaty also gave Cape Brenton Island and Ile Saint Jean (today's Prince Edward Island) to France.

British settlers established Halifax in 1749, and it became the the capital of Nova Scotia. Many **Protestant** people from France, Germany and Switzerland came to Nova Scotia during the early 1750's in order to escape religious **persecution** in their European homelands.

In 1755, British troops from New England began to force the Acadians who did not **swear allegiance** to Britain out of Nova Scotia. Thousands of these Acadian people fled to Prince Edward Island, Quebec, the French colony of Louisiana, and the British colonies in America.

Five years later, more than 20 ships carrying New Englanders landed on the shores of Nova Scotia. These new arrivals took over the land the Acadians had left. They also established many new settlements. During and after the Revolutionary War in America (1775-1783), about 35,000 *United Empire Loyalists* moved to Nova Scotia. These Loyalists were British colonists in America who refused to fight against Great Britain in the Revolutionary War. Between 1773 and 1850, large numbers of settlers from Scotland and Ireland **migrated** to Nova Scotia.

In 1867, Nova Scotia joined with New Brunswick, Ontario and Quebec in forming the Canadian confederation.

Canoes like this one were the main means of transportation along the St. Lawrence River for the Hudson's Bay Company.

NOVA SCOTIA

Name _____

REVIEW QUESTIONS   Date _____

Circle the correct answer.

1. What year did Nova Scotia become a province?
    a. 1948   b. 1867   c. 1949   d. 1834

2. Who were the first Europeans to settle in the Nova Scotia region?
    a. English   b. French   c. Vikings   d. Spanish

3. Who was probably the first European to visit the Nova Scotia region?
    a. the Micmac   b. John Cabot   c. Sam Champlain   d. Vikings

Fill in the blanks with the correct answer.

4. The capital city of Nova Scotia is _____ .

5. Samuel de Champlain made the first _____ of the
   _____ of Nova Scotia.

6. What did the French call the Nova Scotia region? _____

7. What does Nova Scotia mean? _____
   _____

8. Tell what areas were included in the land that King James I granted to Sir Alexander.
   _____
   _____

9. Why do you suppose the French and English fought so much to control the region?
   _____
   _____
   _____
   _____

Bonus ☆ ☆ ☆

   Use another resource book and write a report about moose or caribou, John Cabot, Eskimos, commercial fishing, Scotland, Port Royal, Latin, Acadians, or Sable Island. Include pictures and maps in your report if they are applicable.

CANADA: Section 8 - 50   © Golden Educational Center

ONTARIO

Map • Facts • History & Review Questions

New Words to Learn:

Find the words in a dictionary and write the meanings on the lines.

1. **bountiful** - _____

2. **frontier** - _____

3. **Jesuit** - _____

4. **legislative** - _____

5. **lieutenant** - _____

6. **mission** - _____

7. **pelt** - _____

8. **permafrost** - _____

9. **prime minister** - _____

10. **raid** - _____

11. **reform** - _____

ONTARIO

CANADA: Section 9 - 52

ONTARIO
(ahn-TAIR-ee-oh)

Name _____

Date _____

BECAME A PROVINCE: July 1, 1867 — one of the four original provinces.

CAPITAL CITY: Toronto.

AREA: 891,189 square kilometers (344,090 square miles).

POPULATION (est. 1990): 9,546,200 people. <u>Density</u>: 11 people per square kilometer. 28 people per square mile. 81% urban (city) living and 19% rural (country) living.

LARGEST CITY: Toronto - 3,427,000 people (Largest in Canada)

ELEVATION: <u>Highest</u>: 693 meters (2,275 feet) above sea level in the Timiskaming District. <u>Lowest</u>: Sea level.

ADDITIONAL INFORMATION: Ontario is the most populated of all Canadian provinces. About one-third of the entire country's population live in Ontario. • Ontario's manufacturing industry is its main source of income. It produces as much as the other nine provinces combined. It also ranks first among the Canadian provinces in farm income. • It is second, only to Quebec, in area. • Ontario extends farther south than the northern border of California. It also extends north where some of the ground beneath the surface is **permafrost**. • The name of the province comes from the Iroquois Indians. The word *Ontario* may mean *beautiful lake*; or it may mean *rocks standing high* or *near the water* — referring to Niagara Falls.

Ontario's Flag

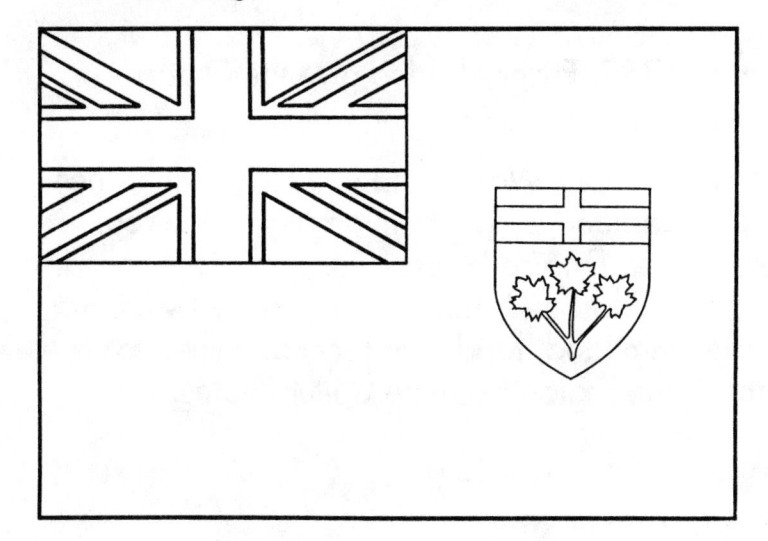

Flag Description

1. The background of the flag is red.
2. The coat of arms is on the right. The three maple leaves symbolize Canada. The bear stands for strength.
3. The British Union Jack is in the upper right corner. The cross at the top of the coat of arms is red on a white background. Both represent the bond with Britain.
4. Color the flag the correct colors.

ONTARIO
"Workshop of the Nation"

Name _____

Date _____

EARLY HISTORY in BRIEF

The first people to live in the Ontario region were Native American Indians. The three main Indian groups were the Chippewa, Huron and the fearless Iroquois. The Chippewa lived in the forests north and east of Lake Superior. They hunted beaver and other small game for food. The Huron Indians lived between Lake Huron and Lake Ontario. They grew most of their food. The Iroquois Indians were great warriors. Both the Chippewa and Huron people feared the wandering groups of Iroquois who often **raided** their homes.

The first white man to explore the Ontario region was Étienne Brulé of France. Samuel de Champlain, founder of Quebec, sent him to report on the region in 1610. Champlain came to the region three years later. He paddled a canoe up the Ottawa River. In 1615, he journeyed farther south into the Lake Huron area. French trappers followed this route into the wilderness to collect the **bountiful** supply of **pelts** in the region. During the 1620's and 1630's, Brulé and other French explorers traveled farther than Champlain. They explored the Lake Superior region, and then pushed on into Lake Michigan and beyond.

French missionaries followed the fur trappers into the Ontario region, to establish some of the first settlements. Fort Sainte Marie was built by **Jesuit** priests in 1639. The fort became the center of a group of **missions**. These missions became known as *Huronia*. They were built among the Huron Indians. In 1648, the Iroquois made war on the Huron Indians and the missionaries. The Iroquois defeated them and destroyed the missions.

In the 1650's and 1660's, French explorers entered the region north of Lake Superior. Their explorations led to the establishment of the Hudson's Bay Company in London, England. Over the years, hundreds of fur traders came to the region to hunt and trap. However, only a few scattered settlements were established near Kingston, Niagara Falls and Windsor.

As a result of losing the Seven Year's War, in 1763, France had to give the Ontario region to Great Britain.

It wasn't until a year after the American Revolutionary War ended in 1783, that further settlement took place. People who were loyal to England began to migrate into the region from the United States. About 6,000 of these *United Empire Loyalists*, as they were called, settled west of the Ottawa River. These loyalists had lost their homes and money by leaving the United States. The British government gave them land, food, livestock, and seed to survive. About 4,000 other settlers also came to the region from the United States.

ONTARIO

Name _____

Date _____

In 1791, the Ontario region became the separate province of *Upper Canada*. Newark (present-day Niagara-on-the-Lake) was made the capital. In 1793, the governor chose to move the capital to York (present-day Toronto). However, the move was not completed until 1797.

Many Americans who either liked **frontier** life or wanted more land settled in the region. Sometimes, even whole communities, such as the Pennsylvania Dutch, moved north.

The War of 1812 between Great Britain and the United States began 21 years after the creation of Upper Canada. More than half of the colony's population were former Americans. However, most of them were loyal to their new homeland. British and Canadian troops, as well as the colonists, stopped United States forces that invaded Upper Canada on several occasions.

In 1825, the Erie Canal linked Lakes Erie and Ontario with New York City. This was the first important national waterway built in the United States. This allowed many people from New York to migrate into Upper Canada.

During the 1830's, citizens of Upper Canada became dissatisfied with the government. They were only allowed to elect the **legislative** assembly. The **lieutenant** governor, who was appointed by the British government, had all of the real power. Demands by the people of Upper Canada for political **reform** were ignored by Britain. In 1837, William Lyon Mackenzie, a political leader, and a small group of followers rebelled. British soldiers stopped the rebellion very quickly. They executed many of the rebels, imprisoned some others, and some, including Mackenzie, escaped to the United States.

After the rebellion, the British government sent the Earl of Durham to investigate the political problems of Upper Canada. He recommended that Upper and Lower Canada (part of present-day Quebec) be united under one government. In 1840, the British government passed the *Act of Union*. The next year, Upper and Lower Canada formed the single province of Canada.

In 1864, leaders from the province of Canada suggested a federal union of all British provinces in eastern North America. All of the provinces except Newfoundland and Prince Edward Island agreed to join the confederation. On July 1, 1867, the *British North America Act* created the *Dominion of Canada*. New Brunswick, Nova Scotia, Ontario and Quebec were the original provinces in the Dominion.

Ottawa was made the federal capital. Sir John A. Macdonald of Ontario became the first **prime minister** of Canada. John S. Macdonald, not related to Sir John A. Macdonald, became the first prime minister of Ontario. ❏

ONTARIO

Name _____

REVIEW QUESTIONS   Date _____

Circle the correct answer.

1. What year did Ontario become a province?
   a. 1948   b. 1840   c. 1867   d. 1864

Fill in the blanks with the correct answer.

2. The capital city of Ontario is _____ . According to _____ it is also Ontario's and _____ _____ city.

3. Samuel de _____ was the _____ of Quebec.

4. What was the name and date of the Act that created the Dominion of Canada?
   _____

5. What does the word *Ontario* mean? _____
   _____

6. Write Ontario's nickname, and tell why you think it was named that.
   _____
   _____

7. Explain why the citizens of Ontario were dissatisfied with the British government. Tell what they did and the result of their actions. (Use more paper if you need to.)
   _____
   _____
   _____
   _____
   _____
   _____

Bonus ☆ ☆ ☆

Use another resource book and write a report on the Iroquois, Chippewa or Huron Indians, the Great Lakes, the Jesuit priests or missionaries, Niagara Falls, Ontario's manufacturing, or the Seven Years War. Include pictures and maps in your report if they are applicable.

PRINCE EDWARD ISLAND
Map • Facts • History & Review Questions

New Words to Learn:
Find the words in a dictionary and write the meanings on the lines.

1. **county** - _____

2. **cradle** - _____

3. **delegate** - _____

4. **economic** - _____

5. **govern** - _____

6. **maritime** - _____

7. **sapling** - _____

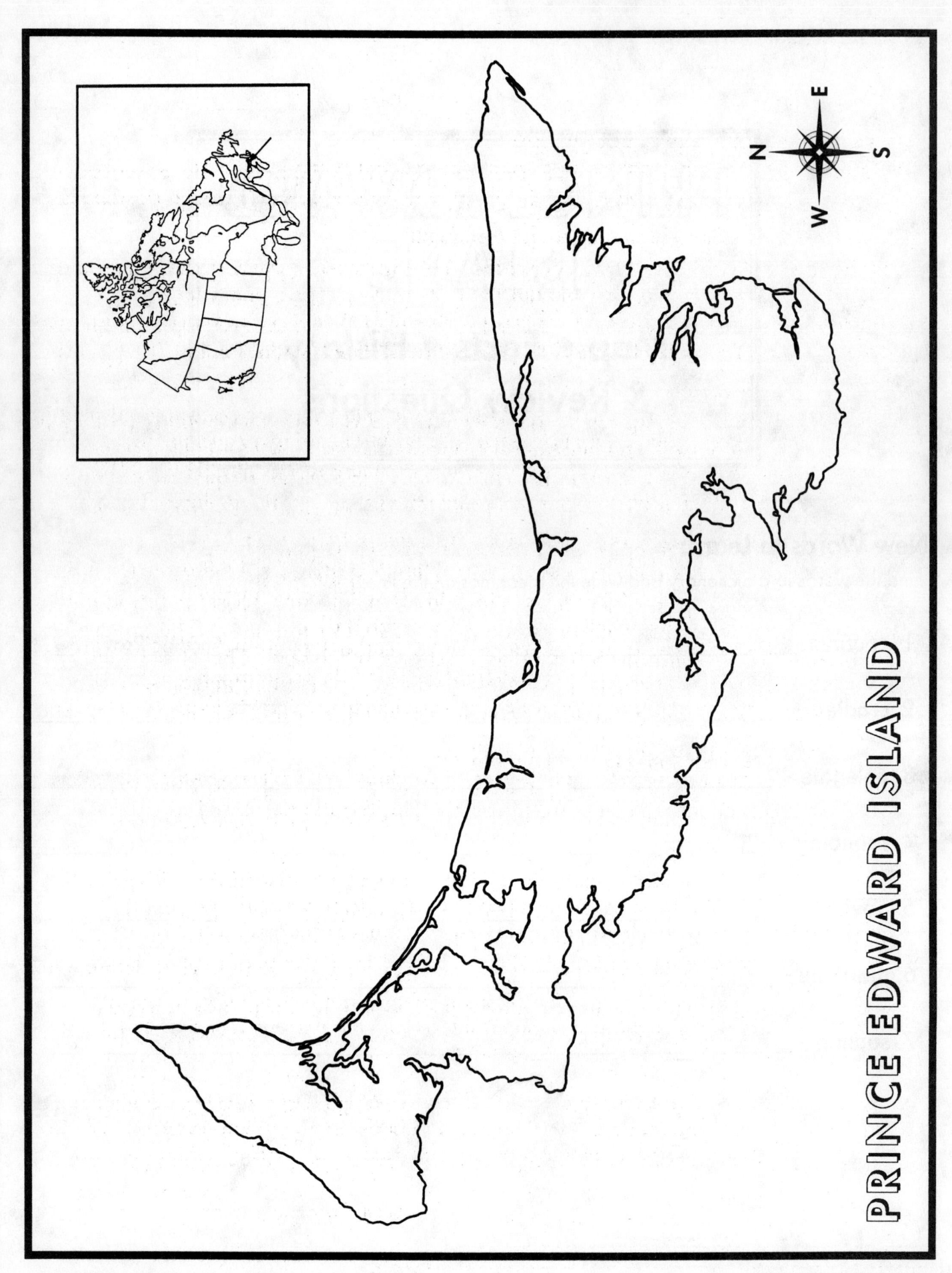

PRINCE EDWARD ISLAND

CANADA: Section 10 - 58

© GOLDEN EDUCATIONAL CENTER

PRINCE EDWARD ISLAND

(PRINS ED-word I-luhnd)

Name _____

Date _____

BECAME A PROVINCE: July 1, 1873 — the 7th province.

CAPITAL CITY: Charlottetown.

AREA: 5,659 square kilometers (2,185 square miles).

POPULATION (est. 1990): 130,000 people.   <u>Density</u>: 23 people per square kilometer
                                                           59 people per square mile.
                                  63% urban (city) living and 37% rural (country) living.

LARGEST CITY: Charlottetown - 15,800 people.

ELEVATION: <u>Highest</u>: 142 meters (465 feet) above sea level in Queens County.
              <u>Lowest</u>: Sea level along the coasts.

ADDITIONAL INFORMATION: Prince Edward Island is one of the four Atlantic Provinces. It is the smallest and most thickly populated of all the Canadian provinces. Its people usually call their province "The Island" or use its initials "P.E.I." • Charlottetown is the only city of The Island. • It is the only province that is completely separated from the mainland of North America. • Prince Edward Island ranks among the leading producers of oysters in Canada as well as the United States.

Prince Edward Island's Flag

Flag Description

1. The background of the flag is white. The border alternates red and white blocks on three sides starting with red at the top.

2. The lion on the top of the flag is gold on a red background. It represents the tie with Great Britain.

3. The three oak **saplings** stand for the three **counties** of Prince Edward Island and the large oak tree represents Canada and Great Britain.

4. Color the flag the correct colors.

© GOLDEN EDUCATIONAL CENTER

CANADA: Section 10 - 59

PRINCE EDWARD ISLAND

"Garden of the Gulf" & "Million Acre Farm"

Name _____

Date _____

EARLY HISTORY in BRIEF

The Micmac Indians inhabited the region of Prince Edward Island long before any white people arrived on the island. The Micmac Indians called the island *Abegweit*, which means **cradled** *on the waves*.

The first known white man to visit the island was the French explorer Jacques Cartier. His ship arrived in the waters near the island on June 30, 1534. Another French explorer, Samuel de Champlain, claimed the island for France in 1603. He named the island *Ile St. Jean* (Isle St. John).

It took one hundred, seventeen years after Champlain named the island before French colonists began to settle on the island. They established the first French colonies near present-day Charlottetown and Georgetown.

In 1758, during the Seven Years War (also known as the French and Indian War 1754-1763), British troops seized control of the area. At the end of the war, and as a result of being defeated, France gave the island to Great Britain. Britain changed its name to St. John's Island and made it a part of Nova Scotia.

The island's location, being separated from the Canadian mainland, made it very difficult to **govern**. In 1769, St. John's Island became a separate British colony. The British changed its name to *Prince Edward Island* in 1799.

In 1851, the British allowed the colonists to govern their own affairs. In 1864, **delegates** from Prince Edward Island, New Brunswick and Nova Scotia met in Charlottetown to discuss forming a **Maritime** union (union of these Maritime colonies). Delegates from present-day Ontario and Quebec joined the meeting and proposed a federal union of all of the provinces. The same delegates met a second time in 1864 in Quebec. In the second meeting, the plan for a Canadian union was written. This plan led to the creation of the *Dominion of Canada* on July 1, 1867.

Prince Edward Island refused to join the Dominion. The Island was enjoying a period of great **economic** prosperity, and felt they did not need to be a part of the union. The people also feared that the larger provinces would control their small island in the new Dominion. However, an economic depression soon developed, and the people realized they needed help. Prince Edward Island joined the Dominion as the 7th province on July 1, 1873.

PRINCE EDWARD ISLAND

REVIEW QUESTIONS

Name _____

Date _____

Circle the correct answer.

1. What year did Prince Edward Island become a province?
   a. 1873　　　b. 1967　　　c. 1949　　　d. 1864

2. Who was probably the first European to visit the Prince Edward Island region?
   a. D. Micmac　　b. J. Cabot　　c. S. Champlain　　d. J. Cartier

3. Who was the first European to name Prince Edward Island?
   a. D. Micmac　　b. J. Cabot　　c. S. Champlain　　d. J. Cartier

Fill in the blanks with the correct answer.

4. The capital city of Prince Edward Island is _____. It is also the _____ city of _____.

5. Prince Edward Island is one of the world's leading producers of _____.

6. France had to give The Island to _____ as a result of their _____ in the _____ War.

7. What was the original name of The Island? _____

8. Explain why Prince Edward Island did not join the Dominion at first.
   _____
   _____

9. Explain what happened in 1864 in Charlottetown.
   _____
   _____
   _____
   _____

Bonus ☆ ☆ ☆

Use another resource book and write a report on Samuel de Champlain, Jacques Cartier, Prince Edward or oysters.
Include pictures and maps in your report if they are applicable.

QUEBEC

Map • Facts • History & Review Questions

New Words to Learn:

Find the words in a dictionary and write the meanings on the lines.

1. **civil** - _____

2. **custom** - _____

3. **tradition** - _____

4. **valid** - _____

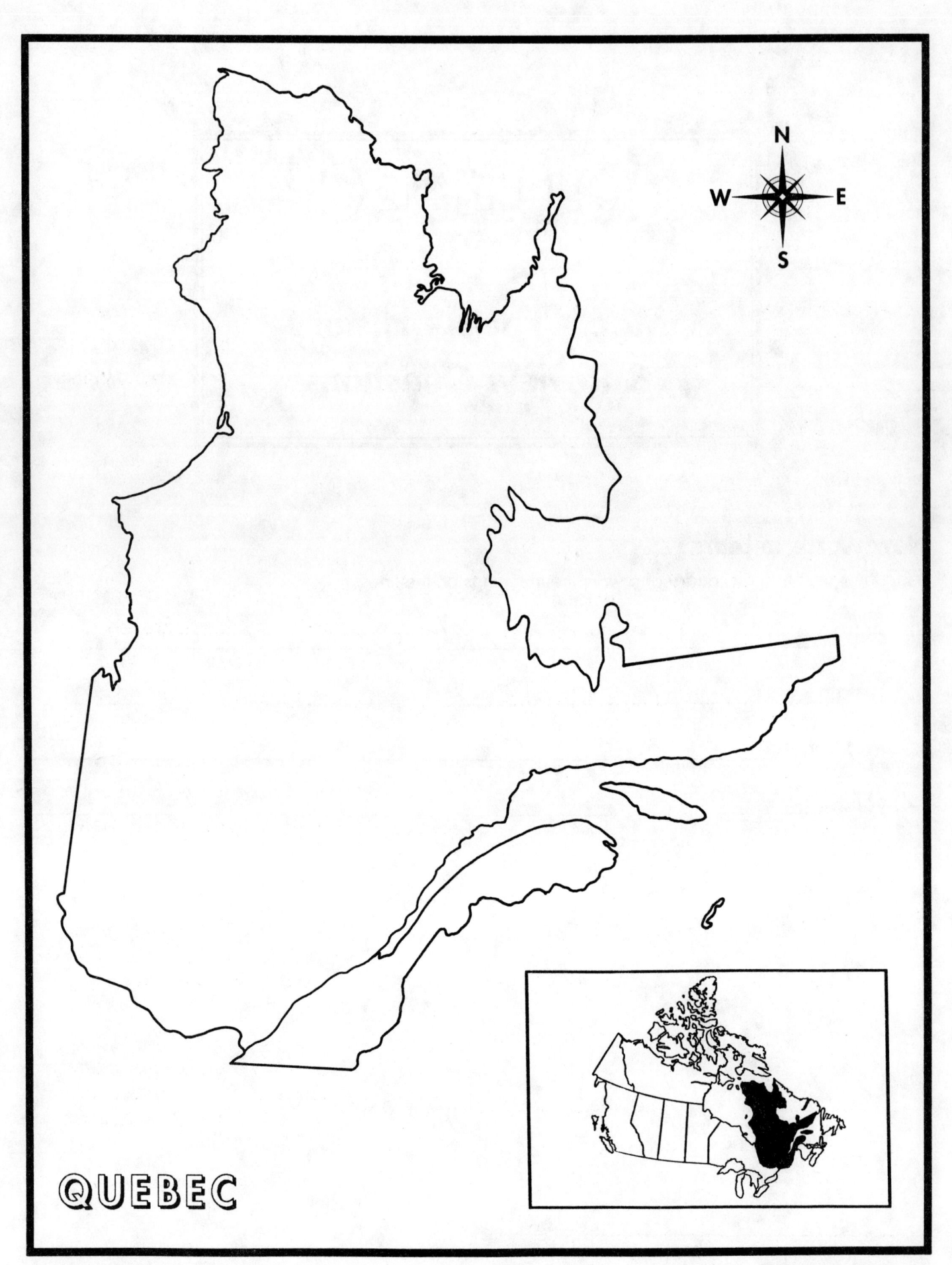

QUEBEC

CANADA: Section 11 - 64

QUEBEC
(kwee-BECK or kay-BECK)

Name _____

Date _____

BECAME A PROVINCE: July 1, 1867 — one of the four original provinces.

CAPITAL CITY: Quebec.

AREA: 1,356,789 square kilometers (523,859 square miles).

POPULATION (est. 1990): 6,679,000 people.   <u>Density</u>: 5 people per square kilometer.
13 people per square mile.
79% urban (city) living and 21% rural (country) living.

LARGEST CITY: Montreal - 2,921,000 people.

ELEVATION: <u>Highest</u>: Mont d'Iberville - 1,646 meters (5,400 feet) above sea level.
<u>Lowest</u>: Sea level.

ADDITIONAL INFORMATION: Quebec is the largest province of Canada, and ranks second among the provinces in population. About 80 percent of the people have French ancestors, and most of this group speak only French. These French Canadians write the name of the province as *Québec*. Montreal is the second largest French-speaking city in the world — Paris is the largest. • The French influence in Quebec makes it different from the rest of Canada. The people mostly follow the **customs** and **traditions** of France, rather than Great Britain. • Today, many people living in Quebec want the province to become politically independent from Canada. The debate over Quebec's separation has created tension between Quebec and the other provinces.

Quebec's Flag

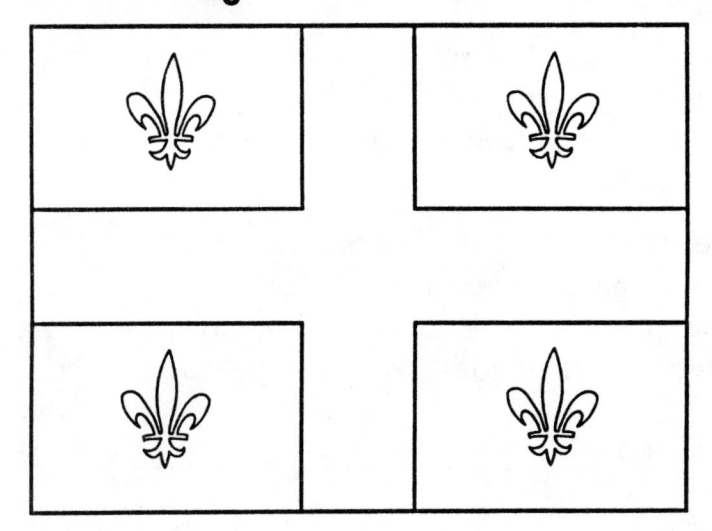

Flag Description

1. In the center of each of the four rectangles on the flag is a *fleur-de-lis*. Each is white on a blue background.

2. The cross in the middle is white. It stands for the cross planted by Jacques Cartier who reached the Gulf of the St. Lawrence River in 1534.

3. Color the flag the correct colors.

© GOLDEN EDUCATIONAL CENTER

CANADA: Section 11 - 65

QUEBEC
"Storied Province"

Name _____

Date _____

EARLY HISTORY in BRIEF

The first people to inhabit the region of Quebec were Native American Indians and Eskimos. The Eskimos lived in the far north and mainly to the west of Ungava Bay along the shores of Hudson Bay. The Naskapi Indians lived in the eastern part of the Quebec region. They primarily hunted for their food. The members of the Naskapi tribe who lived toward the south were called *Montagnais* (mountaineers) by the French people who eventually settled in the region. Five tribes of the Iroquois nation made permanent homes along the Richelieu River and west of it.

Cree Indians moved between the Naskapi and Eskimo lands and south of James Bay. Other American Indian tribes that lived in the Quebec region included the Algonquin, Micmac, Malecite and Huron.

In 1534, Jacques Cartier was the first European to reach the Gulf of Saint Lawrence. He claimed the surrounding region of Quebec for France. Another French explorer, Samuel de Champlain, explored the Saint Lawrence River in 1603. In 1608, he founded the settlement of Quebec City. This was the first permanent settlement in all of Canada. He also arrived at the lake that was named after him, and explored the interior as far as Georgia Bay on Lake Huron. Montreal, originally named *Ville Marie*, was founded as a missionary center in 1642.

Fur-trading companies controlled Quebec for more than 60 years. In return for their trading rights, the companies were supposed to bring settlers into the region. One of the most powerful trading companies was the *Hudson's Bay Company* of London, England.

In 1663, the king of France, Louis XIV, made Quebec a province of France. By 1760, there were tens of thousands of French Settlers in Quebec. They became the ancestors of most of the French Canadians of today.

French settlers fought off and on with various tribes of Indians in Quebec until the 1700's. In 1672, Louis de Buade, Comte de Frontenac, was appointed governor of Canada (called *New France*). He and Jean Baptiste Talon sent out many expeditions that expanded the French empire in the region of Quebec.

French and English colonists fought over the rich fur trade in Quebec during the first years of settlement in the region. The conflict became a large-scale conflict about 1689. As a result of the *Treaty of Utrecht*, Great Britain gained control of the Mainland of Nova Scotia, Newfoundland, and the Hudson Bay region. The longest period of peace followed the treaty, and lasted for the next thirty years.

QUEBEC

Name _____

Date _____

Fighting for control of the Quebec region (and all of Canada) between France and Great Britain began again in the mid-1700's. The final struggle for control of the region began in 1754. (This struggle is known in the United States as the *French and Indian War*, and in Europe and Canada as the *Seven Years' War*.) French forces were winning until 1758, when British soldiers seized important French positions. In 1759, the British defeated the French forces in the Battle of Quebec, at Quebec City. The French governor surrendered the colony in 1760, after three British armies closed in on Montreal. France gave Canada, including Quebec, to the British in 1763, at the *Treaty of Paris*.

For the first four years after the British took control of the region, Canada was under military rule. The British made very few changes during this period, as they did not want to upset the conquered French Canadian settlers. However, in 1667, Canada was renamed the *Province of Quebec*.

The British government at first proposed that they be governed by the same laws they had in England. However, British law, at that time, did not allow Roman Catholics to vote, or hold public office. At that time, most French Canadians were Roman Catholic, and very few British Protestants had moved to the region. A change in this law came in 1774 with the passing of the *Quebec Act*. This act guaranteed freedom of religion to French Canadians and made French **civil** law **valid** in British courts.

After Great Britain lost the Revolutionary War against the United States, *loyalists* (colonists who remained loyal to Britain) left the Untied States. They settled in the southwestern part of the old province of Quebec, and in what are now known as the *Atlantic Provinces*. The British divided Quebec into two regions in 1791 — *Upper and Lower Canada*. Loyalists lived near the Great Lakes and the upper Saint Lawrence River. This region was called *Upper Canada*. Today it is Ontario. The French Canadians lived along the lower Saint Lawrence River in *Lower Canada*. This area is today's Quebec.

Because of Canadians' unrest over the way they were being ruled by Great Britain, the British passed the *Act of Union of 1840*. This act united Upper and Lower Canada (sometimes called *Canada West* And *Canada East* after the passing of the Act) into the new *Province of Canada*.

In October, 1864, a conference with representatives from the provinces was held at Quebec City. They wanted to unite all of the provinces under one government. This Quebec Conference of 1864 turned out to be a constitutional convention. The representatives almost called the new government the *Kingdom of Canada*. However, they finally decided on *Dominion*. In 1867, The *British North American Act* was made law. This act established the provinces of Ontario and Quebec; uniting these with New Brunswick and Nova Scotia to form the *Dominion of Canada*. ❑

QUEBEC

Name _____

REVIEW QUESTIONS

Date _____

Circle the correct answer.

1. What year was Quebec city founded?
   a. 1604   b. 1608   c. 1867   d. 1864

2. Who made Quebec a province in 1663?
   a. Britain   b. France   c. Vikings   d. Hudson's Bay Company

3. Who was probably the first European to visit the Quebec region?
   a. the Eskimo   b. John Cabot   c. Samuel Champlain   d. Jacques Cartier

Fill in the blanks with the correct answer.

4. The capital city of Quebec is _____ . According to population, _____ is Quebec's _____ city. Quebec is also called _____ . It is the oldest _____ in all of Canada.

5. Explain what delegates debated (and the result) at the *Quebec Conference*.
   _____

6. Why didn't the British make changes right after taking control of Quebec?
   _____
   _____

7. Tell your feelings and what you would do if you were living in Quebec and were conquered by another country.
   _____
   _____
   _____
   _____

Bonus ☆ ☆ ☆

Use another resource book and write a report on the Iroquois, Cree or Naskapi Indians, Eskimos, the Treaty of Utrecht, France, Loyalists, Quebec Act, or Samuel de Champlain. Include pictures and maps in your report if they are applicable.

SASKATCHEWAN

Map • Facts • History & Review Questions

New Words to Learn:
Find the words in a dictionary and write the meanings on the lines.

1. **petroleum** - _____

2. **uranium** - _____

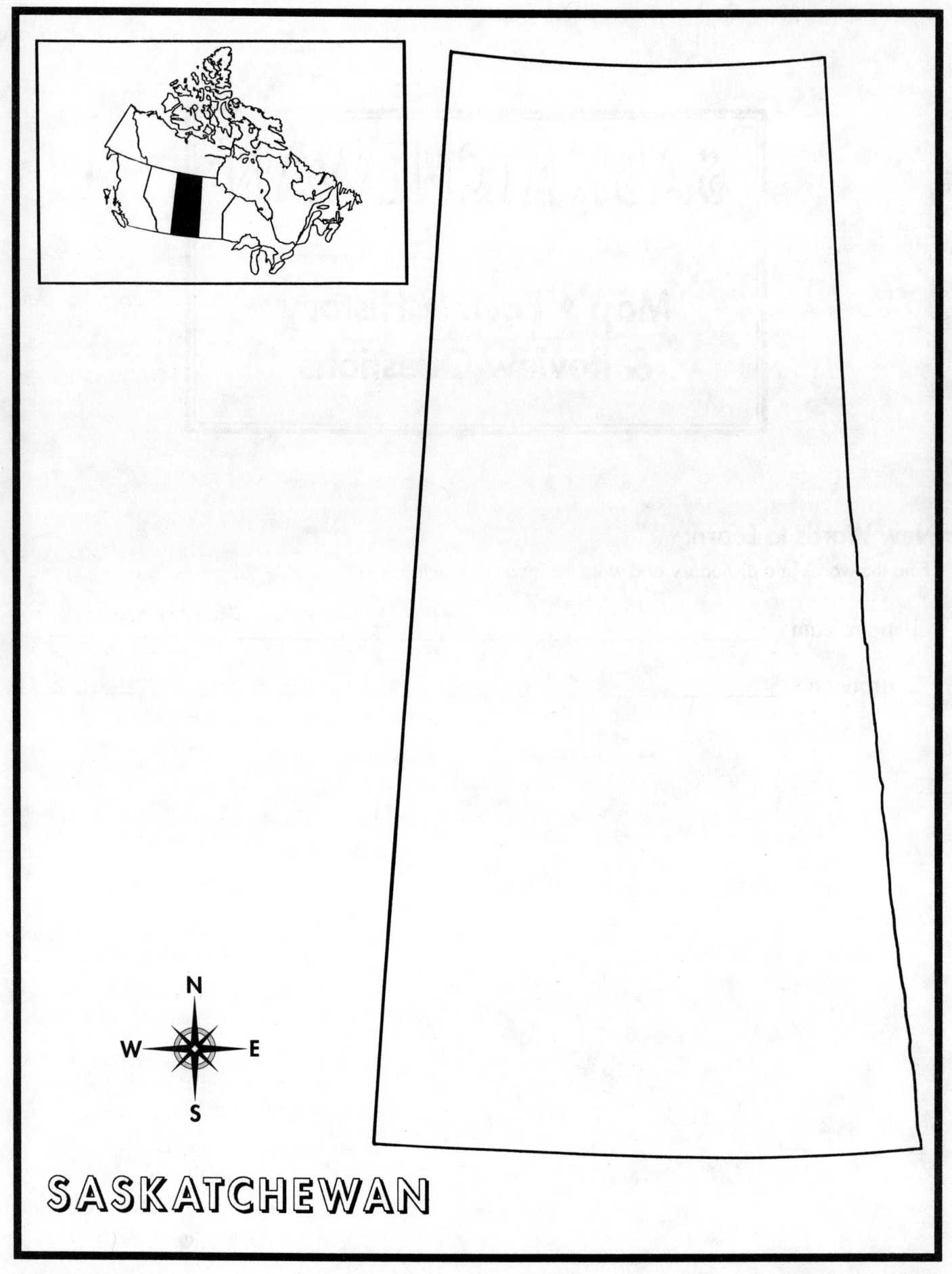

SASKATCHEWAN

CANADA: Section 12 - 70

SASKATCHEWAN
(sas–KACH–uh–wahn)

Name _____

Date _____

BECAME A PROVINCE: September 1, 1905 — the 9th province.

CAPITAL CITY: Regina.

AREA: 570,699 square kilometers (220,348 square miles).

POPULATION (est. 1990): 1,007,100 people. _Density_: 2 people per square kilometer. 5 people per square mile. 56% urban (city) living and 44% rural (country) living.

LARGEST CITY: Saskatoon - 177,700 people.

ELEVATION: _Highest_: 1,392 meters (4,567 feet) above sea level in the Cypress Hills.
Lowest: Lake Athasbasca - 213 meters (700 feet) above sea level.

ADDITIONAL INFORMATION: Saskatchewan is one of Canada's Prairie Provinces. • It is the greatest wheat-growing region in all of North America. The province has about two-thirds of the farmland in Canada. • In the 1950's, oil was discovered in the southern part of the province. Today, it produces about one-eighth of Canada's **petroleum**, and is the leading oil producer of North America. It also produces about half of Canada's **uranium**. • The province took its name from the river named by the Cree Indians. They called the winding river _Kisiskadjewan_ or _Kis-is-ska-tche-wan_, which means _fast flowing_ or _river that turns around when it runs_.

Saskatchewan's Flag

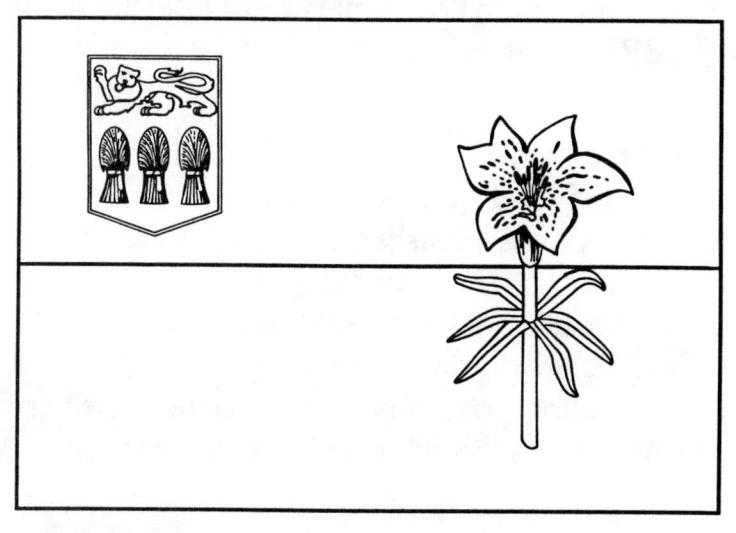

Flag Description

1. The top half of the flag is green and represents Saskatchewan's forests.//
2. The bottom half is gold and symbolizes the wheat fields.
3. The Prairie Lily is in the center. It is the Provincial flower of Saskatchewan.
4. The coat of arms is in the top left corner. The lion represents England and the wheat is a major crop.
5. Color the flag the correct colors.

SASKATCHEWAN
"Canada's Breadbasket"

Name _____

Date _____

EARLY HISTORY in BRIEF

The first people to live in the region of today's Saskatchewan were the Chipewyan, Assiniboine and Plains Cree Indians. The Chipewyan lived north of the Churchill River. The Assiniboine in the southern area, in the valleys of the Assiniboine and Saskatchewan rivers. The Plains Cree lived in the area between these two peoples. All three of these tribes lived by hunting.

It was in 1670, that King Charles II of England granted fur-trading rights in the Saskatchewan region to the Hudson's Bay Company of London. The Saskatchewan region was only a part of the vast territory called *Rupert's Land*, that was granted to the company.

White men were not known to enter the Saskatchewan region until 1690. That year, the Hudson's Bay Company sent Henry Kelsey on an expedition to find new trapping grounds. Kelsey spent two years with the Indians living in the region. He brought back reports of large numbers of fur-bearing animals to the company.

A French-Canadian fur trader named Pierre Gaultier de Varennes, Sieur de la Vérendrye, left Montreal with his sons in 1731. They were trying to find an overland route to the Pacific Ocean. During the journey, La Vérendrye's sons built trading posts along the Saskatchewan River in the early 1740's. The Hudson's Bay Company did not fund more exploration until 1754, when Anthony Henday crossed the region on his way to the Rocky Mountain foothills.

Samuel Hearne of the Hudson's Bay Company built the Cumberland House on Cumberland Lake in 1774. This was the company's first trading post built in the interior of Rupert's Land. The post became the first permanent white settlement in the Saskatchewan region. In the late 1770's, some fur traders from Montreal established the North West Company to compete with the Hudson's Bay Company. Both companies were operating trading posts in the Saskatchewan region until 1821. That year the North West Company combined with the Hudson's Bay Company.

In 1870, the newly formed *Dominion of Canada* acquired all of Rupert's Land from the Hudson's Bay Company. Canada paid the company $1,500,000 and allowed the company to keep large areas of the plains. Canada also established the North West Territories, which included the former Rupert's Land, in 1870. They reorganized the Territories five years later. In 1882, the Canadian government divided part of the Territories into districts. Two of these districts, Saskatchewan and Assiniboia, made up most of what is today's Saskatchewan. In 1905, the Canadian government created the province of Saskatchewan. It entered the Dominion with Alberta as the 8th and 9th provinces.

SASKATCHEWAN

Name _____

REVIEW QUESTIONS   Date _____

Circle the correct answer.

1. What year did Canada acquire the Saskatchewan region?
    a. 1870   b. 1905   c. 1949   d. 1690

2. When did the first white men come to the Saskatchewan region?
    a. 1870   b. 1905   c. 1949   d. 1690

3. Who was probably the first European to visit the region?
    a. H. Kelsey   b. S. Champlain   c. Sir Hudson   d. La Vérendrye

Fill in the blanks with the correct answer.

4. The capital city of Saskatchewan is _____ .

5. Who were the first to live in the Saskatchewan region?
   _____

6. What does Saskatchewan produce the most of in all of North America?
   _____

7. Explain why La Vérendrye left Montreal. _____
   _____

8. Explain why the first permanent settlement was built in the Saskatchewan region.
   _____
   _____

9. Why do you suppose the Hudson's Bay Company stopped funding exploration of the Saskatchewan region?
   _____
   _____
   _____

Bonus ☆ ☆ ☆

Use another resource book and write a report on the Chipewyan Indians, Henry Kelsey, Rupert's Land, the Cumberland House, Northwest Passage, Samuel Hearne, or the La Vérendryes. Include pictures and maps in your report if they are applicable.

NORTHWEST TERRITORIES

Map • Facts • History & Review Questions

New Words to Learn:
Find the words in a dictionary and write the meanings on the lines.

1. **Arctic Circle** - _____

2. **document** - _____

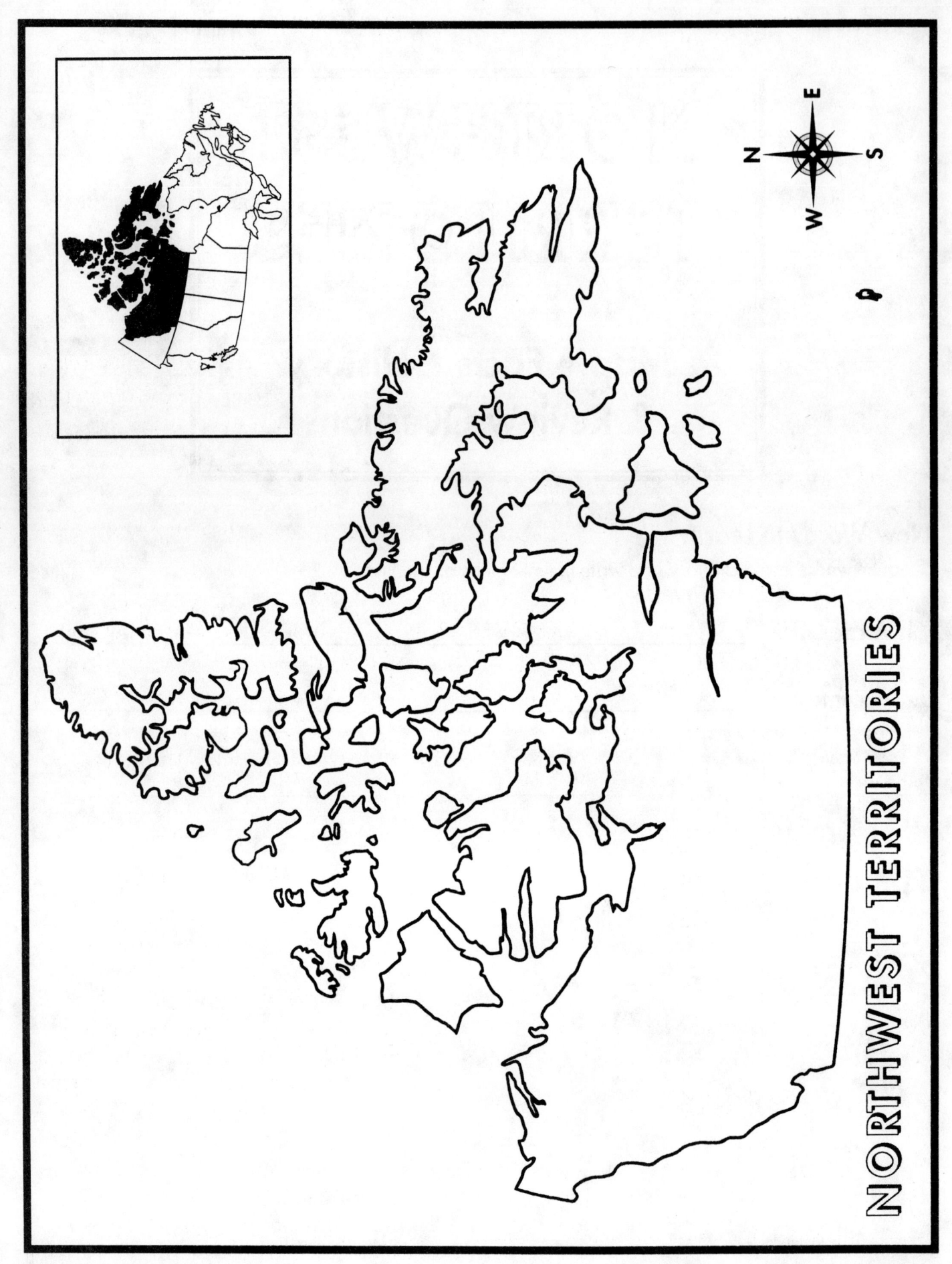

NORTHWEST TERRITORIES

CANADA: Section 13 - 76

© Golden Educational Center

NORTHWEST TERRITORIES

Name _____

Date _____

BECAME A TERRITORY: Acquired in 1870. Present boundaries were established in 1912.

CAPITAL CITY: Yellowknife.

AREA: 3,293,020 square kilometers (1,271,442 square miles).

POPULATION (est. 1990): 53,100 people. *Density*: 1 person per 62 square kilometers. 1 person per 24 square miles. 50% urban (city) living and 50% rural (country) living.

LARGEST CITY: Yellowknife - 11,800 people.

ELEVATION: *Highest*: Mt. Sir James MacBrien - 2,762 meters (9,062 feet) above sea level. *Lowest*: Sea level along the coast.

ADDITIONAL INFORMATION: Northwest Territories is a huge area that covers about one-third of Canada. Its northernmost region is only 800 kilometers (500 miles) from the North Pole. About half of the Northwest Territories lies within the **Arctic Circle**. • The Northwest Territories is divided into three geographical districts. • Until the 1950's, the Territories were one of the world's last undeveloped frontiers. • The region has only one railroad and three major highways. • All of the islands in Hudson, James and Ungava bays are part of the Northwest Territories.

Northwest Territories' Flag

Flag Description

1. The flag is divided into three vertical panels. The panels on the left and right are blue. They represent the skies and waters.

2. The center panel is white, for the snows. The coat of arms is in the middle of the center panel. The fox stands for the fur industry. The bars of gold stand for the minerals.

3. Color the flag the correct colors.

© Golden Educational Center

CANADA: Section 13 - 77

NORTHWEST TERRITORIES

Name _____

Date _____

EARLY HISTORY in BRIEF

Long before any Europeans came to the Northwest Territories region, Eskimos and Indians called the region home. Most of the Eskimos lived in the interior of Keewatin, around the shores of Hudson Bay, Baffin Island and in the Arctic coast region. Almost all of the Indians lived in what is today's District of Mackenzie. Today, even as hundreds of years ago, most of these Indians make their living by hunting and trapping.

Viking sailors were probably the first Europeans to visit the Northwest Territories region. Historians believe they may have sighted the Arctic shores about A.D. 1000. However, no **documented** records have been discovered of any such sighting.

The European explorers who followed Christopher Columbus soon realized that North America was not part of the Asian continent. At this time, most of the countries financing exploration expeditions were only interested in traveling to Asia for the rich trade. They wanted to find an easy route to Asia more than explore and settle in North America. For this reason, they began to look for a *Northwest Passage*, or waterway that would take them around or through the North American continent. Martin Frobisher, was the first documented white person to discover any part of the Northwest Territories. He was an English sailor who reached the coast of Baffin Island in 1576. He claimed the vast region the property of Great Britain. Britain named the region *Rupert's Land*.

Until 1770, all of the expeditions of the region traveled by ship. Samuel Hearne, of the Hudson's Bay Company, was the first white man to cross the Territories by land. In 1770, he set out from Churchill in present-day Manitoba. He traveled overland until he reached the mouth of Coppermine River in 1771. He also explored the Great Slave Lake region on his return journey. Sir Alexander Mackenzie also traveled overland and reached the Mackenzie River in 1789.

The Hudson's Bay Company was granted control of the Northwest Territories region by King Charles II of England. In 1870, the newly formed Dominion of Canada acquired Rupert's Land from the Company. At the same time, it obtained a region called the *North West Territory* from Great Britain. This North West Territory was the land north, west and south of Rupert's Land. The Canadian government organized these newly acquired areas into the North West Territories, which later became known as the *Northwest Territories*.

The Territories lost part of the Manitoba region in 1870, when Manitoba became a province. The Yukon Territory was divided from it in 1898. The provinces of Alberta and Saskatchewan were taken from it in 1905. In 1912, Manitoba and Quebec acquired more area from the Territories. ❑

NORTHWEST TERRITORIES

Name _____

Date _____

REVIEW QUESTIONS

Circle the correct answer.

1. What year did the first Europeans probably visit the Northwest Territories region?
   a. 1494   b. 1770   c. 1000   d. 1576

2. Who were the first Europeans to visit the Northwest Territories region?
   a. Englishmen   b. Frenchmen   c. Vikings   d. Spaniards

3. What region is located to the west of the Northwest Territories?
   a. Ontario   b. Alberta   c. Yukon   d. Hudson Bay

Fill in the blanks with the correct answer.

4. The capital city of the Northwest Territories is _____ .

5. Samuel Hearne was the first _____ to cross the _____ by land.

6. What did the English first call the Northwest Territories region?
   _____

7. The Northwest Territories was one of the world's last _____
   _____ .

8. Explain why so many European explorers visited North America after Columbus.
   _____
   _____
   _____
   _____
   _____
   _____

Bonus ☆ ☆ ☆

Use another resource book and write a report on the Vikings, Eskimos, Rupert's Land, the Arctic, Northwest Passage, Samuel Hearne, or Sir Alexander Mackenzie. Include pictures and maps in your report if they are applicable.

© golden educational center   CANADA: Section 13 - 79

YUKON TERRITORY
Map • Facts • History & Review Questions

New Words to Learn:
Find the words in a dictionary and write the meanings on the lines.

1. **annually** - _____

2. **deposit** - _____

3. **extinct** - _____

4. **prospector** - _____

5. **tributary** - _____

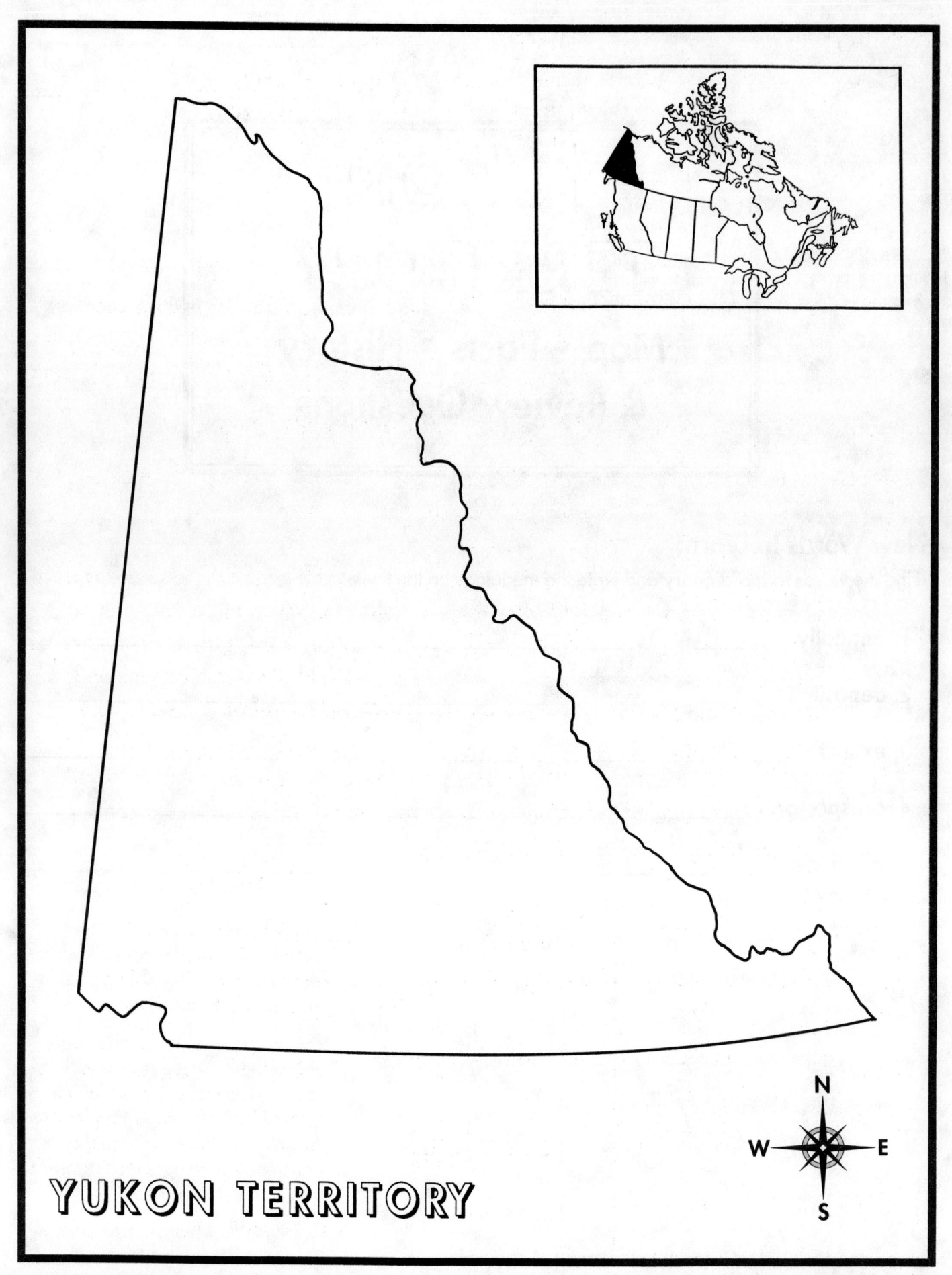

YUKON TERRITORY

CANADA: Section 14 - 82

© Golden Educational Center

YUKON TERRITORY
(YOO–kahn)

Name _____

Date _____

BECAME A TERRITORY: 1898.

NATION'S CAPITAL CITY: Whitehorse.

AREA: 478,969 square kilometers (184,931 square miles)

POPULATION (est. 1990): 25,700 people.   *Density:* 1 person per 19 square kilometers.
                                                          1 person per 7 square miles.
                                            61% urban (city) living and 39% rural (country) living.

LARGEST CITY: Whitehorse - 15,200 people.

ELEVATION: *Highest:* Mount Logan - 5,950 meters (19,520 feet) above sea level.
              Lowest: Sea level along the Beaufort Sea.

ADDITIONAL INFORMATION: Yukon Territory a region in northwest Canada, and is about one-third the size of Alaska. • The largest mountain system of North America almost covers all of the Yukon Territory. Mount Logan is the highest peak in all of Canada. • The lowest temperature ever recorded in North America was –63° C (–81 F.), at Snag Airport near the Alaska border on February 3, 1947. The Territory's record high temperature was 35° C (95° F.), on June 18, 1950. • The Yukon River flows through the Territory. It is one of the longest rivers in North America. • The word *Yukon* probably came from the Indian word *Youcon* — which means *greatest* or *big river*.

Yukon Territory's Flag

Flag Description

1. The left panel is green for the forests. The middle panel is white for the snows. The right panel is blue for the Yukon River.

2. The coat of arms is in the middle above the fireweed, the official flower. The wavy line is blue for the Yukon River. The red triangles are for the mountains. The gold bars stand for the mineral resources. The cross at the top is red.

3. Color the flag the correct colors.

© GOLDEN EDUCATIONAL CENTER

CANADA: **Section 14 - 83**

YUKON TERRITORY

Name _____

Date _____

EARLY HISTORY in BRIEF

Eskimo and other Native American Indians were the first people to live in the region of today's Yukon Territory. Historians believe the Eskimo people originally migrated from Siberia to Alaska thousands of years ago. They later spread across Arctic North America all the way to Greenland. The Vikings who landed on the shores of Greenland in about A.D. 1100 probably encountered some Eskimo people. Some Eskimos live farther north than any other people. The Eskimo often ate their food raw. In fact, the word *Eskimo* comes from an American Indian word meaning *eaters of raw meat*. The Eskimos called themselves *Inuit* or *Yuit*. Both words mean *people*. The way of life for the Canadian Eskimos changed very little until 1950. That is when fur-trading and the number of caribou sharply declined.

Robert Campbell, a British fur trader of the Hudson's Bay Company, came to the Yukon region in the 1840's. He was the first known white man to visit the region. He named the Pelly River and part of the Yukon River which he called *Lewes*. The Lewes was renamed the *Yukon* in 1949. In 1848, he built a trading post on the Pelly River at Fort Selkirk. However, the Chilkat Indians destroyed the fort a short time after it was built. The Yukon region was a part of the Hudson's Bay Company's fur-trading empire until 1870, when it was made part of the Northwest Territories.

Gold was discovered on Bonanza Creek on August 17, 1896. Bonanza Creek is a **tributary** of the Klondike River, near the present site of Dawson. It was discovered by George Carmack and his Indian friends Skookum Jim and Tagish Charlie. This discovery led to the Klondike Gold Rush of 1897 and 1898. Thousand of **prospectors** came to the Yukon after news of the discovery reached the rest of the world. In 1990, over $22 million worth of gold came out of the area. Even today, gold worth over $8 million is **annually** mined from the rich **deposits**.

Many of the miners in the Yukon were often rough and unruly. Many North-West Mounted Police (now the *Royal Canadian Mounted Police*) were sent to the region to preserve order. The large number of prospectors who migrated to the Yukon region increased its political importance. In 1898, the Yukon became a territory, and Dawson was made its capital.

At the height of the Klondike Gold Rush in 1898, about 35,000 people lived in the Yukon Territory. Whitehorse had railroad service and became the distributing point of supplies for the entire territory. Because of this, it grew more rapidly than Dawson. Whitehorse was made the capital of the Yukon Territory in 1951.

Buffalo hunting is prohibited by law to save them from extinction.

CANADA: Section 14- 84

© GOLDEN EDUCATIONAL CENTER

YUKON TERRITORY

Name _____

REVIEW QUESTIONS   Date _____

Circle the correct answer.

1. What year did the Yukon become a territory?
    a. 1898   b. 1897   c. 1896   d. 1951
2. Who were the first Europeans to settle in the Nova Scotia region?
    a. French   b. English   c. Vikings   d. Spanish
3. Who was probably the first European to visit the Yukon region?
    a. the Eskimo   b. R. Pelly   c. R. Campbell   d. M. Klondike

Fill in the blanks with the correct answer.

4. The capital city of the Yukon territory is _____ .
   However, the Yukon's first capital was _____ .

5. What does the word Yukon probably mean?
   _____

6. Why did Whitehorse grow more rapidly than Dawson?
   _____
   _____

7. Why were the Mounties sent to the Yukon region when it only had a few thousand people living there?
   _____
   _____
   _____

8. What is a prospector?
   _____
   _____
   _____

Bonus ☆ ☆ ☆

Write a story about you as a prospector in the Yukon. Tell where you were from; how you got there; what you did while you were there; and when you left. Be as creative and detailed as you can. Include pictures and maps in your report if they are applicable.

© Golden Educational Center

CANADA
Answer Keys

Section 1 - Extra Maps (page 1)
All maps are *Teacher Check*

Section 2 - Canada (page 14)
1. Toronto
2. Canada; New Brunswick; Nova Scotia; Ontario
3. French; English
4. Iceland; first; A.D. 1000
5. 1931
6. *Teacher Check*
7. *Teacher Check*
8. *Teacher Check*
9. New France; Province of Quebec; Dominion of Canada; Kingdom of Canada (optional)

CANADA

REVIEW ANSWERS

Section 3 - Alberta (page 20)
1. d. King Charles II
2. a. Rupert's Land
3. a. 1914
4. Blackfoot; southern prairies; foothills.
5. Sarcee; allies
6. Fort Macleod
7. Hudson's Bay Co.; North West Co.
8. $1.5 million
9. *Teacher Check*
10. *Teacher Check*

Section 4 - British Columbia (page 26)
1. Vancouver
2. United States; treaty; 49th parallel
3. third
4. Victoria-Vancouver
5. 1858
6. *Teacher Check*
7. *Teacher Check*
8. *Teacher Check*
9. *Teacher Check*

Section 5 - Manitoba (page 32)
1. a. Sir Button
2. d. 1870
3. a. 1783
4. Winnipeg; population; largest
5. Henry Kelsey; Hudson's Bay Co.; fur
6. Chipewyan; Woods Cree; Plains Cree; Assiboin; Chippewa
7. producing high quality wheat and grain
8. *Teacher Check*

Section 6 - New Brunswick (page 38)
1. d. 90%
2. d. 1867
3. d. United States
4. Fredericton
5. 1534; 70 years
6. Acadia
7. Canada's first incorporated city
8. *Teacher Check*

Section 7 - Newfoundland (page 44)
1. c. 1949
2. b. 1855
3. b. Vikings
4. St John's
5. *Teacher Check*; Europeans; Vikings; A.D. 1000; Vikings; Hemisphere; Christopher Columbus
6. fighting & disease
7. *Teacher Check*

Section 8 - Nova Scotia (page 50)
1. b. 1867
2. b. French
3. b. John Cabot
4. Halifax
5. accurate map; coast
6. Acadia
7. New Scotland
8. *Teacher Check*
9. *Teacher Check*

CANADA

REVIEW ANSWERS

Section 9 - Ontario (page 56)
1. c. 1867
2. Toronto; population; Canada's; largest
3. Champlain; founder
4. British North American Act – July 1, 1867
5. Beautiful Lake or rocks standing high or near the water
6. *Teacher Check*
7. *Teacher Check*

Section 10 - Prince Edward Island (page 61)
1. a. 1873
2. d. J. Cartier
3. c. S. Champlain
4. Charlottetown; only or largest; PEI (or The Island)
5. oysters
6. Britain; defeat (or loss); Seven Year's War (or French & Indian War)
7. Ile. St. John (or Isle St. John)
8. *Teacher Check*
9. *Teacher Check*

Section 11 - Quebec (page 68)
1. b. 1608
2. b. France
3. d. Jacques Cartier
4. Quebec; Montreal; largest; Quebec City; permanent settlement
5. *Teacher Check*
6. *Teacher Check*
7. *Teacher Check*

Section 12 - Saskatchewan (page 73)
1. a. 1870
2. d. 1690
3. a. Henry Kelsey
4. Regina
5. Chipewyan; Assiniboine; Plains Cree;
6. wheat and petroleum
7. *Teacher Check*
8. *Teacher Check*
9. *Teacher Check*

Section 13 - Northwest Territories (page 79)
1. c. 1000
2. c. Vikings
3. c. Yukon
4. Yellowknife
5. white man; Territories (or NW Territories)
6. Rupert's Land
7. underdeveloped frontiers
8. *Teacher Check*

Section 14 - Yukon Territory (page 85)
1. a. 1898
2. b. English
3. c. Robert Campbell
4. Whitehorse; Dawson
5. greatest or big river
6. *Teacher Check*
7. *Teacher Check*
8. *Teacher Check*

© GOLDEN EDUCATIONAL CENTER

Golden Educational Center

G.E.C. PUBLICATIONS

"LEADING THE WAY IN CREATIVE EDUCATIONAL MATERIALS"™

Country Study Materials

These books have a section on each of the independent countries of North and South America. Each section has a large country map, a page of current facts and interesting information, a short one or two page history through independence and one page of questions that can be answered with the information we provide. There is also an answer key for each section.

GEC-1965	**NORTH AMERICA Country Studies** (96 pages)	**$9.95**
GEC-1975	**SOUTH AMERICA Country Studies** (96 pages)	**$9.95**

The layout and information of these books are similar to North and South America. Each country or province has its own respective section. **Your kids will love the easy–to–use format!**

GEC-1935	**FAR EAST Country Studies** (112 pages)	**$10.95**
GEC-1936	**MIDDLE EAST Country Studies** (112 pages)	**$10.95**
GEC-1985	**CANADA Province Studies** (96 pages)	**$9.95**

U.S. Outline Maps & State Studies

This 112 page book has an individual Fact Sheet and Outline Map for each of the 50 states, Washing-ton D.C., and the entire U.S. U.S. Waterway and State Bound-ary Maps are also included. The question and research activity pages can be used with each of the states.

GEC-1992   **$9.95**

U.S. Geography

The sections of this 80 page book include a World Overview, Physical, Economical, and Political Features as well as Climate information. Maps, activities and questions are included in each section. There is even a review section for the entire book. **This book has a unique, easy-to-use (and read) format that you and your students will enjoy!**

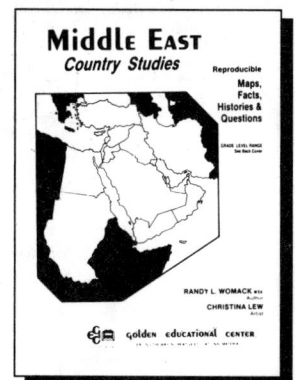

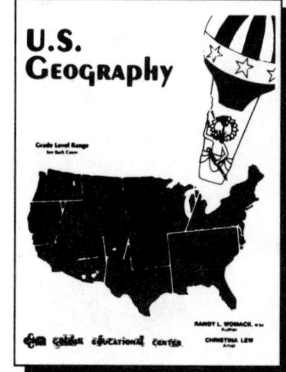

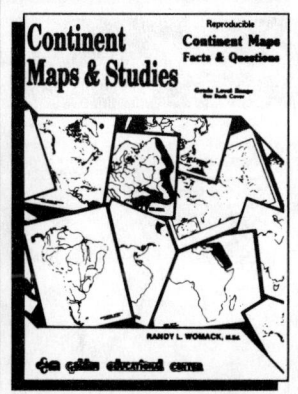

GEC-1993   **$8.95**

Continent Maps & Studies

This book contains an Outline, Waterway, and Political Boundary Map and Individual Fact Sheet for all of the continents. There are questions, research activities and a glossary that can be used with each of continent section. World Maps and answer Keys are also included.

GEC-1905   **$6.95**

Learning the Continents

Africa, Asia, Europe, North America and South America each have a 16 page section of maps & activities. Students use maps to identify, memorize and locate the countries, waterways, and points of interest on each continent. A word search is also included.

GEC-1906   **$9.95**

"JUMBO" REPRODUCIBLE MAPS

These 11x17" maps are printed on card stock.

Continent Maps

GEC-1998 - 1 each of 8 Outline Maps

GEC-1999 - 1 each of 8 Political Boundary Maps
U.S. • N. America • Europe • Africa • S. America • Asia • Australia • World.
$10.00 per package

GEC-1996 - North America Political Boundaries Pack
N. America • Canada • United States • Mexico - Central America

GEC-1997 - Eastern Continents Political Boundaries Pack
World (Pacific View) • Asia • Far East • Middle East
$5.95 per package

U.S. Word Search and State Studies

This 112 page book has a large word search map for each state. Each state also has an interesting fact and short history sheet that can be used to facilitate more research about the respective state.

GEC-1915   **$9.95**

Golden Educational Center

G.E.C. PUBLICATIONS

"LEADING THE WAY IN CREATIVE EDUCATIONAL MATERIALS"™

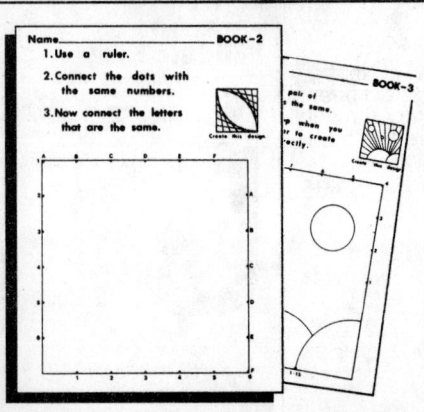

Creating Line Designs

Students use a straight edge to sequentially connect dots in order to create geometric designs. These activities develop visual perception & eye-hand coordina-tion as they build the students' self-confidence. **Your students will love doing these activities!**

GEC-1001	Book-1	........K-1st
GEC-1002	Book-2	.....1st-5th
GEC-1003	Book-3	.....3rd-6th
GEC-1004	Book-4	.....4th-7th

$5.95 each

Story Problems Made Easy

Paring down to the most essential information, students can now see and understand the most important elements of a story problem. **These might be the greatest stories ever told!**

GEC-1101	Book 1	- Sums to 20
GEC-1102	Book 2	- Sums to 99
		(No Carrying/Borrowing)
GEC-1103	Book 3	- Sums to 122
		(With Carrying/Borrowing)

$5.95 each

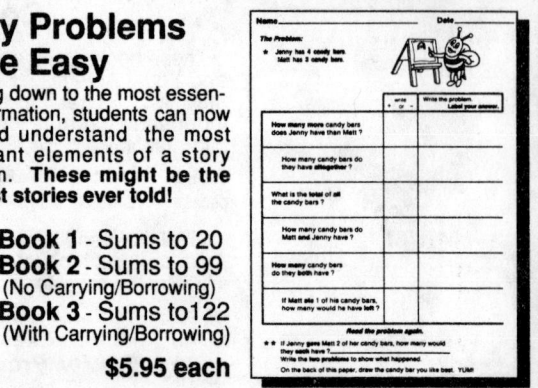

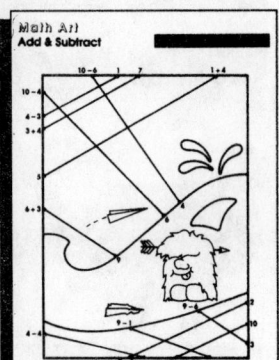

Beginning Math Art

These terrific new books show students the fundamentals of design while they practice solving their math problems. Young students will enjoy doing the 20 activity pages in each of these books

GEC-1013	Add & Subtract	0 to 10
GEC-1014	Add & Subtract	11 to 20
GEC-1015	Multiply & Divide	0 to 12

$5.95 each

Designs in Math $5.95

Students love to create geometric designs by connecting dots and letters between problems and the correct answers. Each book contains 20 pages with one design per page.

GEC-1006	Addition	.....2nd-6th
GEC-1007	Subtraction	.....2nd-6th
GEC-1008	Multiplication	.....3rd-6th
GEC-1009	Division	.....3rd-7th
GEC-1010	Fractions	.....4th-8th
GEC-1011	Equiv. Frac-Dec	...5th-8th

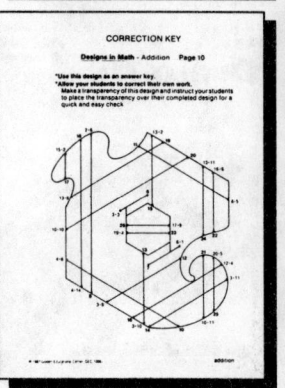

Exciting *New!* Ecology and Art Activities

Ecology Math

Students are presented with simplified ecological information. They then write their ideas on how they can help the ecological situation. The lessons continue with mathematical problems referring to the information first given. Seventeen math lessons with 17 discussion/information sheets in all.

4th and above

GEC-1105 $6.95

Ecology Activities

Teachers discuss the simplified ecology information given in each of the 18 activities with their students. Children are asked to think of things they might be able to do to help with the problem being discussed. There is an art activity to go with each lesson.

Preschool – 3rd

GEC-1205 $5.95

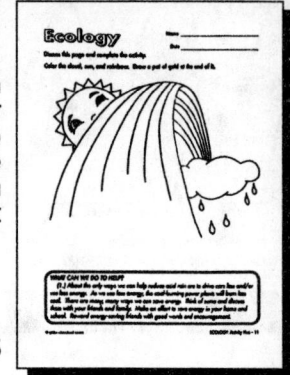

Holiday Greeting Cards

This book has 20 activities where children can create holiday greeting cards for friends and family. Students experiment with several different art media. Teachers love these activities because everything they need is easily obtainable, inexpensive and requires very little preparation.

Preschool – 3rd

GEC-1201 $5.95

Creating Calendars

Children complete an art activity for each month of the year as well as a calendar grid. They can practice writing their numbers or just cutting and pasting. This book is easy to use and materials are inexpensive and easily obtainable.

K – 3rd

GEC-1202 $5.95